"I have not seen a better resource for training... of the gospel. It communicates both to the new Christian and to the seasoned pastor, much like the gospel itself."

Dr. Darrin Patrick, Founder of The Journey, St. Louis, MO; author of *Church Planter: The Man, The Message, The Mission*

"The phrase 'gospel-centered' has become a popular buzzword in Christianity. But just because you talk about the gospel doesn't mean you're being transformed by it. I'm familiar with both Serge and the authors of *The Gospel-Centered Life*, and I know they are profoundly aware, first and foremost, of their own need for gospel renewal. That's why I'm so excited to recommend this material to pastors, leaders, and Christians everywhere who long to see gospel transformation in themselves and in their churches."

Daniel Montgomery, Lead Pastor, Sojourn Church, Louisville, Kentucky

"I've used *The Gospel-Centered Life* in two different church contexts— one in an established church in a Sunday school setting, the other in a smaller, re-start church context in our small groups. The curriculum has a rare combination of being gloriously simple for leaders to use and also having thoughtful and probing content. GCL starts the right conversations, pressing people to push past surface behaviors to the internal world that Jesus so valued. In a culture (and a church) full of people who are skimming through life, GCL presses you to pay attention to the conversations in your head and the motives in your hearts, and to bring all of it under the lordship of Christ and into contact with the power of the gospel. It is easy to use and strikes the rare blend of being applicable and accessible to both the seasoned believer as well as the person considering faith for the first time. We found doing it in all our small groups created a church-wide conversation that had real impact in terms of people's discipleship and understanding of how great the gospel truly is."

Alex Kirk, Lead Pastor, Chatham Community Church, Chapel Hill, NC

"As we seek to make disciples of Jesus, I am continually looking for resources which rightly emphasize true heart-change over mere behavioral-modification. *The Gospel-Centered Life* is one of the most effective tools we are using in that regard."

Brian McCurry, Small Groups Pastor, Fellowship Memphis, Memphis, TN

"We have used *The Gospel-Centered Life* on our Summer Projects, in our discipleship groups on campus, in our small groups at church, and personally among our staff. It has proven to be a very effective way to both ground new believers in an understanding of the richness of the gospel as well as highlight its implications in their lives. In short, it's a home run."

Mike Jackson, Regional Director, Campus Outreach, Central Illinois

"Working with young people brings many unique challenges and adventures that can only be truly impacted by the gospel of Christ. *The Gospel-Centered Life* has helped draw these issues out of our relationships in surprisingly practical ways by going deep quickly enough to grip our affections, yet broad enough to connect with all types of students."

Kenny Hayes, Campus Outreach Director, Bradley University, Grace Presbyterian Church, Peoria, Illinois

THE GOSPEL-CENTERED LIFE

Robert H. Thune and Will Walker

Study Guide with Leader's Notes

New
Growth
Press

www.newgrowthpress.com

The Gospel-Centered Life: Study Guide with Leader's Notes

Copyright © 2009 by Serge

Published 2011 New Growth Press, Greensboro, NC 27404

Editorial Team: Susan Lutz, Patric Knaak, Barb Moseley
Design: Brett Westervelt
Typesetting: Lisa Parnell, lparnell.com
Cover Design: Faceout Books, faceout.com

ISBN: 978-1-942572-91-6 (Print)
ISBN: 978-1-942572-92-3 (eBook)

Printed in Canada

25 24 23 22 21 20 19 18   5 6 7 8 9

CONTENTS

Leader's Guide 81

INTRODUCTION

ABOUT SERGE

Serge never set out to write and publish curriculum. We are an international mission-sending organization that has always believed the power and motive for mission is the gospel of grace at work in the life of a believer. However, along the way, we've also discovered that it's a lot harder to do cross-cultural, team-oriented ministry than we thought. Eventually, we started writing material to keep the gospel front and center in our own lives and relationships. Before long we had pastors and ministry leaders requesting gospel-centered materials for use in their churches and ministries.

Over the years, it's been our privilege to partner with friends who share our passion for the way the gospel transforms both believers and unbelievers alike. This study is the result of one such partnership. Bob Thune and Will Walker wrote *The Gospel-Centered Life* to help their church grow in the gospel. We're partnering with them to publish it because we think it may do the same for you.

Some of the content has been adapted from earlier Serge materials. If you are familiar with *Sonship, Gospel Identity, Gospel Growth,* and *Gospel Love,* you may recognize a few key themes and concepts. If you haven't heard them presented before, Bob and Will have done a great job of articulating the gospel in simple, deep, and transformative ways here. One of the strengths of this curriculum is the way that their experience of church-planting influenced the development of *The Gospel-Centered Life,* which is just one of the reasons that we're so pleased to make it available.

As a cross-denominational, reformed, sending agency with over 200 missionaries in over 25 teams on 5 continents, Serge is always looking for people who are ready to take the next step in a missional lifestyle.

If you'd like to learn more about our teaching, healing, and equipping ministries around the world and what might be right for you, please visit us at http://www.serge.org/mission. If you'd like to learn more about our gospel mentoring programs and the discipleship training that we offer here in the United States, you can find those details at http://www.serge.org/mentoring.

ABOUT THIS STUDY

The Gospel-Centered Life is a 9-lesson small group study intended to help you understand how the gospel shapes every aspect of life. Developed by experienced church-planting pastors, the material is designed to promote transformational conversations among groups of mature Christians, new Christians, and non-Christians. Each lesson is self-contained, featuring clear teaching from Scripture, and requires no extra work outside of the group setting.

THROUGH THE COURSE WE HOPE YOU WILL:

» Deepen your grasp of the gospel as you see your need for continual renewal.

» Grow as you experience transformation from the inside out.

» Be challenged to develop authentic relationships as the gospel moves you to love and serve others.

HOW THIS STUDY IS ORGANIZED

The Gospel-Centered Life contains nine lessons that are grouped around three themes:

What is the gospel?

LESSON 1: THE GOSPEL GRID

If the gospel is constantly "bearing fruit and growing" (Col. 1:6), then everything has to do with the gospel—God, humanity, salvation, worship, relationships, shopping, recreation, work, personality…everything! The objective in this lesson is to establish a framework for talking about the gospel. This framework will get worked out in greater detail over the next two sessions.

LESSON 2: PRETENDING & PERFORMING

Each of us tends to "shrink the cross," which is to say that something is lacking in our understanding, appreciation, or application of Jesus' sacrifice for our sin. This manifests itself in two main ways: pretending and performing. Pretending minimizes sin by making ourselves out to be something we are not. Performing minimizes God's holiness by reducing his standard to something we can meet, thereby meriting his favor. Both are rooted in an inadequate view of God's holiness and our identity.

LESSON 3: BELIEVING THE GOSPEL

We have been focusing on the ways we minimize the gospel—the negative. This lesson turns our attention to the positive: what remedies has God given in the gospel to keep us from shrinking the cross and depending on our own effort?

What does the gospel do in us?

LESSON 4: LAW & GOSPEL

Continue to think about how the gospel interacts with our lives, but now we turn to consider the gospel's relationship to the law. What is the law? Does God expect me to obey it? What is the purpose of the law? How does the law help me to believe the gospel? How does the gospel help me to obey the law?

LESSON 5: REPENTANCE

This lesson deals with repentance. In our culture, this usually sounds like a bad thing, but repentance is the norm for gospel-centered living. Becoming more aware of God's holiness and our sinfulness leads us to repent and believe the gospel of Jesus. Biblical repentance frees us from our own devices and makes a way for the power of the gospel to bear fruit in our lives.

LESSON 6: HEART IDOLATRY

The Christian walk consists of two repeated steps: repentance and faith. Turning our attention to the topic of faith, we focus on how we grow through believing the gospel. This week's goal is to take "believing the gospel" out of the abstract and make it concrete.

How does the gospel work through us?

LESSON 7: MISSION

The gospel is simultaneously at work in us and through us. Inwardly, our desires and motives are being changed as we repent and believe the gospel. As we experience Christ's love in this way, we are compelled to engage those around us with the same kind of redemptive love. God's grace brings renewal everywhere, in us and through us.

LESSON 8: FORGIVENESS

The gospel that works in us always works through us. It shows its power in our relationships and actions. One key way this happens is when we forgive others biblically.

LESSON 9: CONFLICT

Conflict is something we all experience (regularly), but often handle in very fleshly ways. The gospel gives us a pattern and a means to healthy conflict resolution.

HOW TO USE THIS STUDY

The Gospel-Centered Life is designed for small group study, although it is possible to work through the study independently or in a larger group. The tone of the material assumes a small-group format, because this is the setting we've found to be the most effective.

Each of these lessons follows a similar format including these elements…

BIBLE CONVERSATION

We want to start by talking about the Bible together. As the name suggests, this section is designed to stimulate your thinking and prepare you and your group for the ideas that will be presented in each lesson.

ARTICLE

The written articles are the primary source of the teaching content for each lesson. They are short, clear teachings of the concepts being presented in the lesson. Each week, your group will take a few minutes and read the article out loud together.

DISCUSSION

This section is where we communally process the concepts being taught in the article. Often the discussion will work in conjunction with the next section (exercise) to help flesh out the teaching and apply it to our lives in concrete ways.

EXERCISE

Each of the exercises in this study is designed to help you make practical applications of the concepts being taught, or help you understand the content at a deeper heart level. Be sure to allow enough time for your group to adequately work through and discuss the exercises as directed.

WRAP-UP

The wrap-up gives the leader the chance to answer any last minute questions, reinforce ideas, and most importantly spend a few minutes praying as a group.

WHAT TO EXPECT

EXPECT TO BE CHALLENGED...

most of us have reduced the gospel to something much less than it is. As you work through each lesson, expect your thinking about the gospel to be challenged and expanded.

EXPECT THE HOLY SPIRIT...

to be the one ultimately responsible for the growth of your group, and for the change in each person's life—including your own. Relax and trust him.

EXPECT YOUR GROUP'S AGENDA TO INCLUDE...

an open, give-and-take discussion of the article, the questions, and the exercises. Also expect times of prayer at each meeting.

EXPECT STRUGGLE...

and don't be surprised to find that your group is a mixture of enthusiasm, hope, and honesty, along with indifference, anxiety, skepticism, guilt, and covering up. We are all people who really need Jesus every day. So expect your group to be made up of people who wrestle with sin and have problems—people just like yourself!

EXPECT A GROUP LEADER...

who desires to serve you, but who also needs Jesus as much as you do. No leader should be put on a pedestal, so expect that your group leader will have the freedom to share openly about his or her own weaknesses, struggles, and sins.

GOSPEL OVERVIEW

The study you are about to begin aims to help you live a "gospel-centered" life. The obvious question is, What exactly is "the gospel"? That's a question we should clear up before going any further. Though many people are familiar with the word *gospel*, we're often fuzzy about its content.

Many popular "gospel presentations" distill the gospel message down to three or four core principles. These simple summaries can be very helpful. But a richer way to understand the gospel is as a *story*—the true Story that speaks to our purest aspirations and deepest longings. This Great Story has four chapters.

CREATION: THE WORLD WE WERE MADE FOR

The Story begins, not with us, but with God. Deep down, we have a sense that this is true. We sense that we are important—that there is something dignified, majestic, and eternal about humanity. But we also know that we are not ultimate. Something (or Someone) greater than us exists.

The Bible tells us that this Someone is the one infinite, eternal, and unchanging God who created all things out of nothing (Genesis 1:1–31). This one God exists in three persons—Father, Son, and Holy Spirit (Matthew 28:19). Because God is Triune in his being, he wasn't motivated to create the world because he *needed* something—be it relationship, worship, or glory. Rather, he created out of the overflow of his perfection—his own love, goodness, and glory. God made human beings in his image (Genesis 1:27), which is what gives us our dignity and value. He also made us *human*, which means we are created beings, dependent on our Creator. We were made to worship, enjoy, love, and serve him, not ourselves.

In God's original creation, everything was good. The world existed in perfect peace, stability, harmony, and wholeness.

FALL: THE CORRUPTION OF EVERYTHING

God created us to worship, enjoy, love, and serve him. But rather than live under God's authority, humanity turned away from God in sinful rebellion (Genesis 3:1–7; Isaiah 53:6). Our defection plunged the whole world into the darkness and chaos of sin. Though vestiges of good remain, the wholeness and harmony of God's original creation is shattered.

As a result, all human beings are sinners by nature and by choice (Ephesians 2:1–3). We often excuse our sin by claiming that we're "not that bad"—after all, we can always find someone worse than we are! But this evasion only reveals our shallow and superficial view of sin. Sin is not primarily an *action*; it's a *disposition*. It's our soul's aversion to God. Sin is manifested in our pride, our selfishness, our independence, and our lack of love for God and others. Sometimes sin is very obvious and external; other times it's hidden and internal. But "all have sinned and fall short of the glory of God" (Romans 3:23).

Sin brings two drastic consequences into our lives. First, *sin enslaves us* (Romans 6:17–18). When we turn *from* God, we turn *to* other things to find our life, our identity, our meaning, and our happiness. These things become substitute gods—what the Bible calls idols—and they soon enslave us, demanding our time, our energy, our loyalty, our money—everything we are and have. They begin to rule over our lives and hearts. This is why the Bible describes sin as something that "masters" us (Romans 6:14 NIV). Sin causes us to "serve created things rather than the Creator" (Romans 1:25 NIV).

Second, *sin brings condemnation*. We're not just enslaved by our sin; we're *guilty* because of it. We stand condemned before the Judge of heaven and earth. "The wages of sin is death" (Romans 6:23). We are under a death sentence for our cosmic treason against the holiness and justice of God. His righteous anger toward sin stands over us (Nahum 1:2; John 3:36).

REDEMPTION: JESUS COMES TO SAVE US

Every good story has a hero. And the hero of the Gospel Story is Jesus. Humanity needs a Savior, a Redeemer, a Deliverer to free us from the bondage and condemnation of sin and to restore the world to its original good. This Rescuer must be *truly human* in order to pay the debt we owe to God. But he can't be *merely human* because he must conquer sin. We need a Substitute—one who can live the life of obedience we've failed to live, and who can stand in our place to bear the punishment we deserve for our disobedience and sin.

This is why God sent Jesus into the world to be our substitute (1 John 4:14). The Bible teaches that Jesus was fully God—the second person of the Trinity—and also fully human. He was born to a human mother, lived a real flesh-and-blood existence, and died a brutal death on a Roman cross outside Jerusalem. Jesus lived a life of perfect obedience to God (Hebrews 4:15), making him the only person in history who did not deserve judgment. But on the cross, he took our place, dying for our sin. He received the condemnation and death we deserve so that, when we put our trust in him, we can receive the blessing and life he deserves (2 Corinthians 5:21).

Not only did Jesus die in our place, he rose from death, displaying his victory over sin, death, and hell. His resurrection is a decisive event in history; the Bible calls it the "first fruits"—the initial evidence—of the cosmic renewal God is bringing (1 Corinthians 15:20–28). One of the greatest promises in the Bible is Revelation 21:5: "Behold, I am making all things new." All that was lost, broken, and corrupted in the fall will ultimately be put right. Redemption doesn't simply mean the salvation of individual souls; it means the restoring of the whole creation back to its original good.

A NEW PEOPLE: THE STORY CONTINUES

So how do we become a part of the story? How do we experience God's salvation personally and become agents of his redemption in the world? By faith or trust (Ephesians 2:8–9). What does that mean? We trust a taxi driver when we count on him to get us to our destination. We trust a doctor when we agree with her diagnosis and entrust ourselves to her care. And we trust in Jesus Christ when we admit our sin, receive his gracious forgiveness, and rest entirely in Jesus for our acceptance before God. Faith is like getting in the taxi. It's like going under the surgeon's knife. It's a restful, whole-hearted commitment of the self to Jesus (Psalm 31:14–15). This is what it means to believe the gospel.

When we trust in Jesus, we are released from sin's condemnation *and* from its bondage. We are free to say "no" to sin and "yes" to God. We are free to die to ourselves and live for Christ and his purposes. We are free to work for justice in the world. We are free to stop living for our own glory and start living for the glory of God (1 Corinthians 10:31). We are free to love God and others in the way we live, which is the particular focus of this study.

God has promised that Jesus will return to finally judge sin and make all things new. Until then, he is gathering to himself a people "from every nation, tribe, people and language" (Revelation 7:9 NIV). As part of that called-and-sent people, we have the privilege of joining him in his mission (Matthew 28:18–20) as individuals and as part of his spiritual family. By grace, we can enjoy God, live life for his glory, serve humanity, and make his gospel known to others through our words and actions.

This is the good news—the True Story—of the gospel.

THE GOSPEL GRID

BIG IDEA

If the gospel is constantly "bearing fruit and growing" (Col. 1:6), then everything has to do with the gospel—God, humanity, salvation, worship, relationships, shopping, recreation, work, personality…everything! The objective in this lesson is to establish a framework for talking about the gospel. This framework will get worked out in greater detail over the next two sessions, so this lesson is designed to help us understand the concepts and begin exploring how they relate to actual life.

NOTES:

1

THE GOSPEL GRID

"The gospel" is a phrase that Christians often use without fully understanding its significance. We speak the language of the gospel, but we rarely apply the gospel to every aspect of our lives. Yet this is exactly what God wants for us. The gospel is nothing less than "the power of God" (Rom. 1:16). In Colossians 1:6, the apostle Paul commends the Colossian church because the gospel has been "bearing fruit and growing… among [them] since the day [they] heard it." The apostle Peter teaches that a lack of ongoing transformation in our lives comes from forgetting what God has done for us in the gospel (2 Peter 1:3–9). If we are to grow into maturity in Christ, we must deepen and enlarge our understanding of the gospel as God's appointed means for personal and communal transformation.

Many Christians live with a truncated view of the gospel. We see the gospel as the "door," the way in, the entrance point into God's kingdom. But the gospel is so much more! It is not just the door, but the path we are to walk every day of the Christian life. It is not just the means of our salvation, but the means of our transformation. It is not simply deliverance from sin's penalty, but release from sin's power. The gospel is what makes us right with God (justification) and it is also what frees us to delight in God (sanctification). The gospel changes everything!

The following model has been helpful to many people in thinking about the gospel and its implications. This diagram does not say everything that could be said about the gospel, but it does serve as a helpful visual illustration of how the gospel works.

The starting point of the Christian life (conversion) comes when I first become aware of the gap between God's holiness and my sinfulness. When I am converted, I trust and hope in Jesus, who has done what I could never do: he has bridged the gap between my sinfulness and God's holiness. He has taken God's holy wrath toward my sin upon himself.

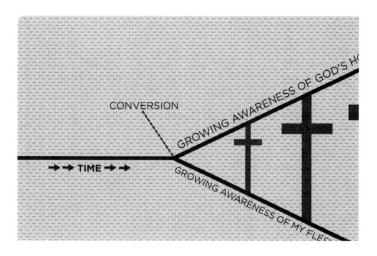

At the point of conversion, however, I have a very limited view of God's holiness and of my sin. The more I grow in my Christian life, the more I grow in my awareness of God's holiness and of my flesh and sinfulness. As I read the Bible, experience the Holy Spirit's conviction, and live in community with other people, the extent of God's greatness and the extent of my sin become increasingly clear and vivid. It is not that God is becoming more holy or that I am becoming more sinful. But my *awareness* of both is growing. I am increasingly seeing God as he actually is (Isa. 55:8–9) and myself as I actually am (Jer. 17:9–10).

As my understanding of my sin and of God's holiness grows, something else also grows: my appreciation and love for Jesus. His mediation, his sacrifice, his righteousness, and his gracious work on my behalf become increasingly sweet and powerful to me. The cross looms larger and more central in my life as I rejoice in the Savior who died upon it.

Unfortunately, sanctification (growth in holiness) doesn't work quite as neatly as we'd like. Because of the indwelling sin that remains in me, I have an ongoing tendency to minimize the gospel or "shrink the cross." This happens when I either (a) minimize God's perfect holiness, thinking of him as something less than his Word declares him to be, or (b) elevate my own righteousness, thinking of myself as someone better than I actually am. The cross becomes smaller and Christ's importance in my life is diminished.

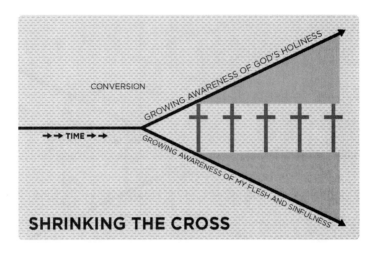

SHRINKING THE CROSS

We'll talk more about the specific ways we minimize the gospel in weeks to come. To counteract our sinful tendency to shrink the gospel, we must constantly nourish our minds on biblical truth. We need to know, see, and savor the holy, righteous character of God. And we need to identify, admit, and feel the depth of our brokenness and sinfulness. We don't need to do these things because "that's what Christians are supposed to do." Rather, we make this our aim because it is the life God wants for us—a life marked by transforming joy, hope, and love.

Growing in the gospel means seeing more of God's holiness and more of my sin. And because of what Jesus has done for us on the cross, we need not fear seeing God as he really is or admitting how broken we really are. Our hope is not in our own goodness, nor in the vain expectation that God will compromise his standards and "grade on a curve." Rather, we rest in Jesus as our perfect Redeemer—the One who is "our righteousness, holiness and redemption" (1 Cor. 1:30).

SIX WAYS OF MINIMIZING SIN

DEFENDING

I find it difficult to receive feedback about weaknesses or sin. When confronted, my tendency is to explain things away, talk about my successes, or justify my decisions. As a result, people are hesitant to approach me and I rarely have conversations about difficult things in my life.

FAKING

I strive to keep up appearances and maintain a respectable image. My behavior, to some degree, is driven by what I think others think of me. I also do not like to think reflectively about my life. As a result, not many people know the real me. (I may not even know the real me.)

HIDING

I tend to conceal as much as I can about my life, especially the "bad stuff." This is different from faking, in that faking is about impressing. Hiding is more about shame. I don't think people will accept or love the real me.

EXAGGERATING

I tend to think (and talk) more highly of myself than I ought. I make things (good and bad) out to be much bigger than they are (usually to get attention). As a result, things often get more attention than they deserve and have a way of making me stressed or anxious.

BLAMING

I am quick to blame others for sin or circumstances. I have a difficult time "owning" my contributions to sin or conflict. There is an element of pride that assumes it's not my fault and/or an element of fear of rejection if it is my fault.

DOWNPLAYING

I tend to give little weight to sin or circumstances in my life, as if they are "normal" or "not that bad." As a result, things often don't get the attention they deserve. They have a way of mounting to the point of being overwhelming.

JUDGING OTHERS

One way to see the value of the Cross Chart is to apply it to a specific area where people commonly struggle. Judging others is something we all do in big and small ways. As a group, brainstorm about some of the specific ways we judge people. The questions below will help you see the connection between judging others and your view of the gospel.

1. What are the specific ways we judge others?

2. Why do we judge others? What reasons do we give for doing this?

3. How do these reasons reflect a small view of God's holiness?

4. How do these reasons reflect a small view of our own sin?

5. Think of a specific person in your life that you are often judgmental toward.

    a. How would a bigger view of God's holiness affect that relationship?

    b. How would a bigger view of your sin affect that relationship?

PRETENDING & PERFORMING

BIG IDEA

This lesson deals with how we "shrink the cross," which is to say that something is lacking in our understanding, appreciation, or application of Jesus' sacrifice for our sin. This manifests itself in two main ways: **pretending** and **performing**. Pretending minimizes sin by making ourselves out to be something we are not. Performing minimizes God's holiness by reducing his standard to something we can meet, thereby meriting his favor. Both are rooted in an inadequate view of God's holiness and our identity.

NOTES:

lesson

ARTICLE

SHRINKING THE CROSS:
PRETENDING & PERFORMING

Last week we looked at a model that illustrates what it means to live in light of the gospel. This week we want to look more closely at the ways we minimize the gospel and reduce its impact in our lives.

Notice that the top line of the chart is labeled "Growing Awareness of God's Holiness." As we stated last time, this does not mean that God's holiness *itself* is increasing, for God is unchangeable in his character. He has always been infinitely holy. Rather, this line shows that when the gospel is functioning correctly in our lives, our *awareness* of God's holy character is constantly growing. We realize in fuller and deeper ways the weight of God's glorious perfections.

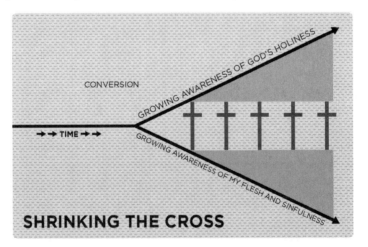

CONVERSION

GROWING AWARENESS OF GOD'S HOLINESS

→ → TIME → →

GROWING AWARENESS OF MY FLESH AND SINFULNESS

SHRINKING THE CROSS

Likewise, the bottom line shows that when the gospel is functioning correctly in our lives, our *awareness* of our own sinfulness is consistently growing. This does not mean that we are becoming more sinful. (In fact, if we're growing in Christ, we'll be starting to see victory over sin.) But we are realizing more and more "how deep the rabbit hole goes" in our character and behavior. We are seeing that we are more profoundly sinful than we first imagined.

As these two lines diverge, the cross becomes larger in our experience, producing a deeper love for Jesus and a fuller understanding of his goodness. At least that's the ideal. But, in reality, because of indwelling sin, we are prone to forget the gospel—to drift away from it like a boat loosed from its moorings. That's why the Bible urges us not to be "moved [away] from the hope held out in the gospel" (Col. 1:23) and to "let the word of Christ dwell in [us] richly" (Col. 3:16). When we are not anchored in the truth of the gospel, our love for Jesus and our experience of his goodness become very small. We end up "shrinking the cross" by either **pretending** or **performing**.

Look again at the bottom line of the chart. Growing in our awareness of our sinfulness is not fun! It means admitting—to ourselves and others—that we are not as good as we think we are. It means confronting what Richard Lovelace called the complex web of "compulsive attitudes, beliefs, and behavior"* that sin has created in us. If we are not resting in Jesus' righteousness, this growing awareness of our sin becomes a crushing weight. We buckle under its load and compensate by **pretending** that we're better than we really are. Pretending can take many forms: dishonesty ("I'm not *that* bad"), comparison ("I'm not as bad as *those* people"), excuse making ("I'm not *really* that way"), and false righteousness ("Here are all the *good* things I've done"). Because we don't want to admit how sinful we really are, we spin the truth in our favor.

Growing in our awareness of God's holiness is also challenging. It means coming face to face with God's righteous commands and the glorious perfections of his character. It means realizing how dramatically we fall short of his standards. It means reflecting on his holy displeasure toward sin. If we are not rooted in God's acceptance of us through Jesus, we compensate by trying to earn God's approval through our **performance**.

---

* Richard Lovelace, *Dynamics of Spiritual Life* (Downers Grove, Ill.: InterVarsity Press, 1979), p. 88.

We live life on a treadmill, trying to gain God's favor by living up to his expectations (or our mistaken view of them).

It's easy to talk about pretending and performing in the abstract. But let's consider how these tendencies find practical expression in our lives.

To discern your subtle tendencies toward pretending, ask yourself this question: *what do you count on to give you a sense of "personal credibility" (validity, acceptance, good standing)?* Your answer to that question will often reveal something (besides Jesus) in which you find righteousness. When we are not firmly rooted in the gospel, we rely on these false sources of righteousness to build our reputation and give us a sense of worth and value. Here are some examples.

> **JOB RIGHTEOUSNESS:** I'm a hard worker, so God will reward me.

> **FAMILY RIGHTEOUSNESS:** Because I "do things right" as a parent, I'm more godly than parents who can't control their kids.

> **THEOLOGICAL RIGHTEOUSNESS:** I have good theology. God prefers me over those who have bad theology.

> **INTELLECTUAL RIGHTEOUSNESS:** I am better read, more articulate, and more culturally savvy than others, which obviously makes me superior.

> **SCHEDULE RIGHTEOUSNESS:** I am self-disciplined and rigorous in my time management, which makes me more mature than others.

> **FLEXIBILITY RIGHTEOUSNESS:** In a world that's busy, I'm flexible and relaxed. I always make time for others. Shame on those who don't!

> **MERCY RIGHTEOUSNESS:** I care about the poor and disadvantaged the way everyone else should.

LEGALISTIC RIGHTEOUSNESS: I don't drink, smoke, or chew, or date girls who do. Too many Christians just aren't concerned about holiness these days.

FINANCIAL RIGHTEOUSNESS: I manage money wisely and stay out of debt. I'm not like those materialistic Christians who can't control their spending.

POLITICAL RIGHTEOUSNESS: If you really love God, you'll vote for my candidate.

TOLERANCE RIGHTEOUSNESS: I am open-minded and charitable toward those who don't agree with me. In fact, I'm a lot like Jesus that way!

These are just a few examples. Perhaps you can think of many more. (Think of anything that gives you a sense of being "good enough" or better than others.) These sources of functional righteousness disconnect us from the power of the gospel. They allow us to find righteousness in what we do instead of honestly confronting the depth of our sin and brokenness. Furthermore, each of these sources of righteousness is also a way of judging and excluding others! We use them to elevate ourselves and condemn those who aren't as "righteous" as we are. In other words, finding righteousness in these things leads us into more sin, not less.

Now, to reveal your tendency toward **performance**, pause and answer this question: *as God thinks of you right now, what is the look on his face?*

Do you picture God as disappointed? Angry? Indifferent? Does his face say "Get your act together!" or "If only you could do a little more for me!" If you imagined God as anything but satisfied because of what Jesus has done for you, you have fallen into a performance mindset. Because the gospel truth is that in Christ, God is deeply satisfied with you. In fact, based on Jesus' work, God has adopted you as his own son or daughter (Gal. 4:7)! But when we fail to root our identity in what Jesus has done for us, we slip into performance-driven Christianity. We imagine that if were "better Christians," God would approve of us more fully. Living this way saps the joy and delight out of following Jesus, leaving us to wallow in a joyless, dutiful obedience. Our gospel becomes very small.

Performance-driven Christianity is actually a minimizing of God's holiness. Thinking we can impress God with our "right living" shows that we've reduced his standards far below what they actually are. Rather than being awed by the infinite measure of his holy perfection, we have convinced ourselves that if we just try hard enough, we can merit God's love and approval.

Our subtle tendencies toward pretending and performing show that failing to believe the gospel is the root of all our more observable sins. As we learn to apply the gospel to our unbelief—to "preach the gospel to ourselves"—we will find ourselves freed from the false security of pretending and performing. Instead we will live in the true joy and freedom promised to us by Jesus. We'll think more about that next time.

RIGHT & WRONG

We have all constructed certain rules or laws that we live by, believing that if we keep them, we are more "right" before God. It is then only a small step before we start judging other people based on their performance regarding these rules or laws. The rules we make for ourselves are usually good things. However, we often abuse them. For example, as we struggle with the desire to be in control of our lives, we erect laws that try to maintain that control. These laws could be as simple as "Don't cut me off the road," or "The house must be kept tidy." When people break these laws, we feel that we are losing control and that people do not respect us. Moreover, we feel that we are right and they are wrong. The usual result is anger, as we try to regain control of the situation and show just how right we are. Thus, instead of the law being used to tell us how we ought to love other people, we use it against other people.

APPLICATION QUESTIONS

1. Give an example of a rule you have made for yourself and others that makes you feel good when it is kept, but irritated or depressed when it is broken.

2. How has your rule-keeping given you a sense of self-righteousness?

3. How does being mastered by this rule keep you from genuinely loving other people? Be specific.

BELIEVING THE GOSPEL

BIG IDEA

We have been focusing on the ways we minimize the gospel—the negative. This lesson turns our attention to the positive: what remedies has God given in the gospel to keep us from shrinking the cross and depending on our own effort?

NOTES:

lesson

3

ARTICLE

BELIEVING THE GOSPEL

In the last two lessons we used a visual illustration to better understand the gospel and the way it functions in our lives. Last time, we considered our propensity to "shrink the cross" by pretending and performing. In this session we want to see how a strong and vibrant belief in the gospel frees us from ourselves and produces true and lasting spiritual transformation.

At the root of the human condition is a struggle for righteousness and identity. We long for a sense of acceptance, approval, security, and significance—because we were designed by God to find these things in him. But sin has separated us from God and created in us a deep sense of alienation. Speaking of the Jewish people in his own day, Paul writes, "[T]hey did not know the righteousness that comes from God and sought to establish their own" (Rom. 10:3). We do the same thing. Theologically speaking, pretending and performing are just two sophisticated ways of establishing our own righteousness. When we pretend, we are making ourselves out to be better than we are. When we perform, we are trying to please God by what we do. Pretending and performing

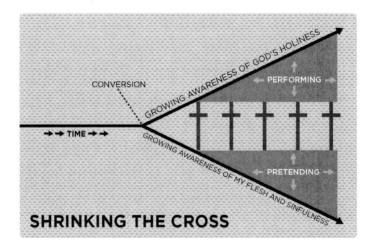

SHRINKING THE CROSS

reflect our sinful attempts to secure our own righteousness and identity apart from Jesus.

To really experience the deep transformation God promises us in the gospel, we must continually repent of these sinful patterns. Our souls must become deeply rooted in the truth of the gospel so that we anchor our righteousness and identity in Jesus and not in ourselves. Specifically, the gospel promises of passive righteousness and adoption must become central to our thinking and living.

Passive righteousness is the biblical truth that God has not only forgiven our sin, but also credited to us Jesus' positive righteousness. Romans 3 speaks of a righteousness from God that comes to us through faith: "But now a righteousness from God, apart from law, has been made known, to which the Law and the Prophets testify. This righteousness from God comes through faith in Jesus Christ to all who believe" (Rom. 3:21–22). Of this passive righteousness, Martin Luther writes:

> It is called "passive righteousness" because we do not have to labor for it.... It is not righteousness that we work for, but righteousness we receive by faith. This passive righteousness is a mystery that someone who does not know Jesus cannot understand. In fact, Christians do not completely understand it and rarely take advantage of it in their daily lives... . When there is any fear or our conscience is bothered, it is a sign that our "passive" righteousness is out of sight and Christ is hidden.
>
> The person who wanders away from "passive" righteousness has no other choice but to live by "works" righteousness. If he does not depend on the work of Christ, he must depend on his own work. So we must teach and continually repeat the truth of this "passive" or "Christian" righteousness so that Christians continue to hold to it and never confuse it with "works" righteousness.*

Luther reminds us that if we "wander away from passive righteousness," our hearts will naturally tend toward self- or works-righteousness. To

---

* Martin Luther, preface to his *Commentary on Galatians*, as quoted in *Sonship* (World Harvest Mission, 2002).

fight against our tendency to shrink the gospel in this way, we must consistently repent of false sources of righteousness and preach the gospel to ourselves, especially the truth of passive righteousness. We must cling to the gospel promise that God is pleased with us because he is pleased with Jesus. When we embrace the gospel in this way, seeing our sin is not scary or embarrassing. It actually leads to worship because Jesus has died for all of it, and it is liberating because we are no longer defined by it! Our righteousness is in Christ. The good news of the gospel is not that God makes much of us, but that God frees us to make much of Jesus.

Adoption is the biblical truth that God has welcomed us into his family as his own sons and daughters by virtue of our union with Jesus. Part of the work of the Holy Spirit is to confirm this adoption within us: "For you did not receive a spirit that makes you a slave again to fear, but you received the Spirit of sonship. And by him we cry, 'Abba, Father.' The Spirit himself testifies with our spirit that we are God's children" (Rom. 8:15–16). Galatians 4:7 says the same thing in different words: "So you are no longer a slave, but a son; and since you are a son, God has made you also an heir."

But just like we wander away from passive righteousness, we are also prone to forget our identity as God's children. We live like orphans instead of sons and daughters. Rather than resting in God's fatherly love, we try to gain his favor by living up to his expectations (or our mistaken view of them). We live life on a treadmill, trying to be "good Christians" so God will approve of us. To fight back against our tendency to shrink the gospel in this way, we must continually repent of our orphan-like mentality and dwell on our true identity as God's sons and daughters. By faith, we must cling to the gospel promise that we are adopted as God's children. Jesus' righteousness has been credited to us apart from works (Rom. 4:4–8). We don't need to do anything to secure God's love and acceptance; Jesus has secured it for us. When we embrace the gospel in this way, the infinite standard of God's holiness is no longer fearful or intimidating. It leads to worship, because Jesus has met it for us. Our identity is in him. The good news of the gospel is not that God favors us because of who we are, but that he favors us in spite of who we are.

At the root of all our visible sins lies the invisible struggle for righteousness and identity. In other words, we never outgrow the gospel. As Martin Luther wrote, "Most necessary is it that we know [the gospel] well, teach it to others, and beat it into their heads continually." As we realize our tendencies toward pretending and performing—our attempts to build our own righteousness and identity—we must repent of sin and believe anew in the promises of the gospel. This is the consistent pattern of the Christian life: repentance and faith, repentance and faith, repentance and faith. As we walk this way, the gospel will take root more deeply in our souls, and Jesus and his cross will become "bigger" in the day-to-day reality of our lives.

lesson

EXERCISE

SELF-ASSESSMENT:
ORPHANS VS. CHILDREN

This is a practical exercise to reveal our sinful tendencies to manipulate life and our daily need to return to Christ. This exercise will humble you, which is one of the first steps in serving Christ and others. Read through each bulleted list. Under "The Orphan," check the box if you see that tendency in yourself. Underline the words that most apply. Under "The Son/Daughter," check the boxes that describe where you most want to grow, underlining the key words.

THE ORPHAN			THE SON/DAUGHTER
Lacks a vital daily intimacy with God	☐	☐	Feels freed from worry because of God's love for you
Anxious about friends, money, school, grades, etc.	☐	☐	Learning to live in a daily partnership with God
Feels as if no one cares about you	☐	☐	Not fearful of God
Lives on a success/fail basis	☐	☐	Feels forgiven and totally accepted
Needs to look good	☐	☐	A daily trust in God's sovereign plan for your life
Feels guilty and condemned	☐	☐	Prayer is a first resort
Struggles to trust things to God	☐	☐	Content in relationships b/c you are accepted by God
Has to fix your problems	☐	☐	Freedom from making a name for yourself
Not very teachable	☐	☐	Is teachable by others
Is defensive when accused of error or weakness	☐	☐	Open to criticism b/c you rest on Christ's perfection
Needs to be right	☐	☐	Able to examine your deeper motives
Lacks confidence	☐	☐	Able to take risks—even to fail
Feels discouraged and defeated	☐	☐	Encouraged by the Spirit working in you
Strong-willed with ideas, agendas, and opinions	☐	☐	Able to see God's goodness in dark times
Solution to failure: "Try harder"	☐	☐	Content with what Christ has provided
Has a critical spirit (complaining and bitterness)	☐	☐	Trusting less in self and more in the Holy Spirit
Tears others down	☐	☐	Aware of inability to fix life, people, and problems
A "competent analyst" of others' weaknesses	☐	☐	Is able to freely confess your faults to others
Tends to compare yourself with others	☐	☐	Doesn't always have to be right
Feels powerless to defeat the flesh	☐	☐	Does not gain value from man-made "props"
Needs to be in control of situations and others	☐	☐	Experiences more and more victory over the flesh
Looks for satisfaction in "positions"	☐	☐	Prayer is a vital, ongoing part of the day
Looks for satisfaction in "possessions"	☐	☐	Jesus is more and more the subject of conversation
Tends to be motivated by obligation and duty, not love	☐	☐	God truly satisfies your soul

LAW & GOSPEL

BIG IDEA

We are still thinking about how the gospel interacts with our lives, but now we are doing it by considering the gospel's relationship to the law. What is the law? Does God expect me to obey it? What is the purpose of the law? How does the law help me to believe the gospel? How does the gospel help me to obey the law? These are the questions before us in this lesson.

NOTES:

THE LAW
& THE GOSPEL

Even a casual reader can see that the Bible is full of commands, prohibitions, and expectations. It tells us what to do and what not to do. These rules or laws often present an obstacle to faith. Non-Christians object to Christianity because it seems like "just a bunch of rules and regulations." And even faithful Christians struggle to understand how the law of God and the gospel of God relate to each other. After all, if we are reconciled to God by grace and not by works, does it really matter whether we obey or not?

When we misunderstand the relationship between law and gospel, it leads to two opposite but equally destructive errors: **legalism** and **license**. Legalists continue to live under the law, believing that God's approval is somehow dependent on their right conduct. Licentious people dismiss the law, believing that since they are "under grace," God's rules don't matter much. These two errors have been around since the days of the apostles. The book of Galatians is written to combat the error of legalism: "Are you so foolish? After beginning with the Spirit, are you now trying to attain your goal by human effort?" (Gal. 3:3). The book of Romans addresses the error of license: "What then? Shall we sin because we are not under law but under grace?" (Rom. 6:15).

Both legalism and license are destructive to the gospel. To avoid these pitfalls, we must understand the biblical relationship between law and gospel. In a nutshell, here's how God designed it to work: the law drives us to the gospel and the gospel frees us to obey the law. Realizing all that God expects of us should drive us in despair to Christ. And once we are united with Christ, the indwelling Holy Spirit causes us to delight in God's law and gives us power to obey it. In his commentary on Romans, Martin Luther summarized it this way: "The law, rightly understood and thoroughly comprehended, does nothing more than remind us of our sin and slay us by it, and make us liable to eternal wrath …. The law is not kept by man's own power, but solely through Christ who pours the Holy Spirit into our hearts. To fulfill the law … is to do its works with pleasure and love…[which are] put into the heart by the Holy Ghost."*

Read that last sentence again: "To fulfill the law…is to do its works with *pleasure* and *love*." Just knowing what God requires is not enough. Obeying him "because it's what we're supposed to do" is not sufficient. Truly fulfilling the law means obeying God out of pleasure and love, because the Holy Spirit lives within us: "I desire to do your will, O my God; your law is within my heart" (Ps. 40:8).

How do we become the kind of people who love God and delight in his law? Answer: through the gospel.

First, it is through the gospel that we become aware of our disobedience to God's law. The first step of the gospel journey is to become aware that "all have sinned and fall short of the glory of God" (Rom. 3:23), and that our disobedience to God's law places us under his curse: "For it is written, 'Cursed is everyone who does not continue to do everything written in the Book of the Law'" (Gal. 3:10).

Second, it is through the gospel that we are freed from the curse of the law. The gospel is the good news that God is willing to forgive us if we turn to Jesus and are justified—declared "not guilty" in God's sight— by faith in him. "Christ redeemed us from the curse of the law by becoming a curse for us, for it is written: 'Cursed is everyone who is hung on a tree.' He redeemed us in order that…through Christ Jesus…by faith we might receive the promise of the Spirit" (Gal. 3:13–14). Jesus has both atoned for our imperfection and attained our perfection through his work on the cross. And by his resurrection, he's freed us forever to live for him (2 Cor. 5:14–15). The law no longer stands in judgment over us. In biblical language, we are no longer "under the law" (Rom. 6:14).

---

* Martin Luther, *Commentary on Romans*, J. Theodore Mueller, trans. (Grand Rapids: Kregel Publications, 2003), pp. xxiii, xv, 110.

Third, it is through the gospel that God sends his indwelling Holy Spirit into us, transforming our hearts and enabling us to truly love God and others. As a result of our justification by faith, "God has poured out his love into our hearts by the Holy Spirit, whom he has given us" (Rom. 5:5). We commonly read the phrase "the love of God" in this verse as God's love for us. But contextually and linguistically this phrase also has the sense of "love from God" or "love for God." Because God loves us, he has poured into our hearts his own capacity to love and delight in himself. Jesus prayed that the very love that God the Father has for his Son would be in us: "I have made you known to them...*in order that the love you have for me may be in them* and that I myself may be in them" (John 17:26).

A true Christian obeys God's law, then, not out of obligation or duty, but out of love, for "love is the fulfillment of the law" (Rom. 13:10). Both legalism and license are fundamentally self-centered. They are not concerned with delight in God or in his law, but with self: "I keep the rules" or "I break the rules." But the gospel frees us from our self-concern and turns us outward. We see that God's law is not constraining but freeing: it is a "law of liberty" (James 1:25 ESV). It is a law that points us to Jesus.

Romans 10:4 says, "Christ is the end of the law for righteousness to everyone who believes" (ESV). In other words, the end, the goal, the point of the law is to drive us to Jesus. When we really "get" what this verse is saying, we begin to see that every command in Scripture points us in some way to Jesus, who fulfills that command for us and in us. He is our righteousness. We no longer need to construct our own.

We are unable to do what the law commands us to do, but Jesus did it for us. And because he lives in us by his Spirit, we are enabled to do it, not from obligation, but from delight. So every command in Scripture points us to our own inadequacy (the bottom line of the Cross Chart), magnifies the good and holy nature of God (the top line of the Cross Chart), and causes us to look to Jesus as the One who forgives our disobedience and enables our obedience. In other words, the law drives us to Jesus and Jesus frees us to obey the law.

4 THE GOSPEL GRID & THE LAW

A "grid" is a pattern for thinking, a filter to run things through, a particular way of looking at something. Understanding the Bible and articulating the gospel in creative, relevant ways involves applying various grids to make sense of truth. In Lesson One we gave you what we call the "gospel grid," illustrated by the Cross Chart. This week we are going to learn how to understand the law of God through that grid.

Every Scripture passage asserts a moral imperative, either explicitly or implicitly. For instance, a verse may tell you not to lie. You can respond to this imperative in three different ways.

> **LEGALISM:** You can try your very best not to lie. This is what it means to live under the law. You will inevitably discover that you cannot not lie, even when you lower your standards about what that means.

> **LICENSE:** You can admit from the start that you cannot obey this command and simply dismiss it as a biblical ideal you are not actually expected to obey. This is what it means to abuse God's grace and give in to sin.

> **GOSPEL:** This is the grid we want to learn. It goes like this:

> **1. God says,** "Do not lie." (Top line of the Cross Chart: God's holiness)

> **2. I cannot obey** this command because I am a sinner. (Bottom line of the Chart: my sinfulness)

3. Jesus did obey this perfectly. (I can point to countless examples in his earthly life as recorded in the Gospels.) Jesus did what I should do (but can't) as my substitute so that God can accept me (2 Cor. 5:17).

4. Because Jesus obeyed the law perfectly and now lives in me, and because I am accepted by God, I am now free to obey this command by his grace and power at work in me.

Applying this grid to your study of the Bible will help you believe the gospel and obey the law without falling into legalism or license. This empowers you to experience the reality that the gospel changes everything.

PRACTICE

Read a passage together and apply this grid. (Pick from Phil. 4:4–7, James 2:1–7, 1 Peter 3:9)

What is the command?

Why can't you do it? (Be specific about your particular struggles to obey this command.)

How did Jesus do this perfectly? (Note specific examples in the Gospels.)

How can God's Spirit in you empower you to obey this command (in specific situations)?

REPENTANCE

BIG IDEA

This lesson deals with repentance. In our culture, this usually sounds like a bad thing—like getting called into the boss's office on Friday afternoon. Far from being bad or unusual, biblical repentance is the norm for gospel-centered living. Becoming more aware of God's holiness and our sinfulness leads us to repent and believe the gospel of Jesus. We are constantly turning from our performing and pretending so that we may live as sons and daughters. Biblical repentance frees us from our own devices and makes a way for the power of the gospel to bear fruit in our lives. But sin taints our repentance and robs us of its fruit. So our aim in this lesson is to (1) expose the ways in which we practice counterfeit repentance and (2) move us toward genuine repentance.

NOTES:

LIFESTYLE REPENTANCE

We have been thinking together about how to consistently live all of life under the influence of the gospel. For the past few weeks, the Cross Chart diagram has served as a visual model to help us understand how the gospel works.

As we have seen, the consistent pattern of the Christian life is repentance and faith. We never stop needing to repent and believe. Jesus' first words in the Gospel of Mark are, "Repent and believe in the gospel" (Mark 1:15). In the first of his Ninety-five Theses, Martin Luther observed, "When our Lord and Master Jesus Christ said, 'Repent'…He willed the entire *life* of believers to be one of repentance." In repentance, we confess our tendency to shrink the cross through performance and pretending. We pull our affections away from false saviors and fraudulent sources of righteousness and turn to Jesus as our only hope.

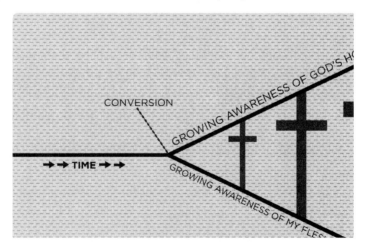

On the surface, repentance seems simple and straightforward, but it's not. Because our hearts are a "factory of idols" (as John Calvin put it), even our repentance can become a vehicle for sin and selfishness. We are skilled practitioners of **false repentance**. One of our greatest needs in gospel-centered living is to understand repentance accurately and biblically.

For most of us, the word *repentance* has a negative connotation. We only repent when we do something *really* bad. The medieval idea of penance often bleeds into our thinking about repentance: when we sin, we should feel really sorry about it, beat ourselves up over it, and do something to make up for it. In other words, repentance often becomes more about *us* than about God or the people we've sinned against. We want to feel better. We want things to be "back to normal." We want to know that we've done our part, so that our guilt is assuaged and we can move on with life.

Think, for instance, about a relationship in which you've spoken hurtful words to someone else. Perhaps your effort at repentance sounded something like this: "I'm sorry I hurt you. I shouldn't have said that. Will you forgive me?" But is this *really* true repentance? Does our sin consist only in the words we've spoken? Didn't Jesus say, "Out of the overflow of [the] heart [the] mouth speaks" (Luke 6:45)?

Though we may have acknowledged our hurtful words, the other person is often feeling the impact of the deeper resentment, anger, envy, or bitterness that lies in our hearts. Unless we confess those sins as well, our "repentance" is not true repentance at all.

How do we start to identify our tendencies toward false repentance? The answer is to look for patterns of *remorse* and *resolution* in our dealings with sin. Remorse: "I can't believe I did that!" Resolution: "I promise to do better next time." Behind this way of living are two great misunderstandings about our hearts. First, we think too highly of ourselves. We do not truly believe the depth of our sin and brokenness (the bottom line of the Cross Chart). This leads us to react in surprise when sin manifests itself: "I can't believe I just did that!" In other words: "That's not what I'm *really* like!" Second, we think we have the power to change ourselves. We think that if we make resolutions or try harder next time, we'll be able to fix the problem.

These patterns of remorse and resolution taint our attitudes toward others as well. Because we think so highly of ourselves, we respond to others' sin with harshness and disapproval. We are very lenient toward our own sin but we resent theirs! And because we think we can change ourselves, we are frustrated when other people aren't changing *themselves* faster. We become judgmental, impatient, and critical.

The gospel calls us to (and empowers us for) **true repentance**. According to the Bible, true repentance:

> **IS ORIENTED TOWARD GOD, NOT ME.** Psalm 51:4: "Against *you, you only*, have I sinned and done what is evil in your sight...."
>
> **IS MOTIVATED BY TRUE GODLY SORROW AND NOT JUST SELFISH REGRET.** 2 Corinthians 7:10: "For godly grief produces a repentance that leads to salvation without regret, whereas worldly sorrow produces death."
>
> **IS CONCERNED WITH THE HEART, NOT JUST WITH EXTERNAL ACTIONS.** Psalm 51:10: "Create in me a clean heart, O God, and renew a right spirit within me" (ESV).
>
> **LOOKS TO JESUS FOR DELIVERANCE FROM THE PENALTY AND POWER OF SIN.** Acts 3:19–20: "Repent, then, and turn to God, so that your sins may be wiped out, that times of refreshing may come from the Lord, and that he may send the Christ who has been appointed for you—even Jesus."

Instead of excusing our sin or falling into patterns of remorse and resolution, true gospel repentance moves us to *realize* and *repent*. Realize: "I *did* do that." ("That IS what I'm really like!") Repent: "Lord, forgive me! You are my only hope." As we learn to live in light of the gospel, this kind of true repentance should become more and more normal for us. We will stop being surprised by our sin, so we will be able to more honestly admit it. And we will stop believing we can fix ourselves, so we will more quickly turn to Jesus for forgiveness and transformation.

Sin is a condition, not just a behavior, so true repentance is a lifestyle, not just an occasional practice. Repentance is not something we do only once (when we are converted), or only periodically (when we feel *really* guilty). Repentance is ongoing, and conviction of sin is a mark of God's fatherly love for us. "Those whom I love I rebuke and discipline. So be earnest, and repent" (Rev. 3:19).

So what are you repenting of?

5

PRACTICING REPENTANCE

We often make excuses for our sin to avoid the hard work of repentance. Below is a list of some common excuses—and (in parentheses) the inner thoughts they reveal. Take a minute to look over the list and then use the questions below to help each other practice genuine repentance.

> » **I was just being honest.** (Can't you handle the truth?)
>
> » **I'm just saying what I feel.** (There's nothing sinful about my feelings.)
>
> » **I was only kidding.** (Didn't you get the joke?)
>
> » **I misunderstood you.** (You're not as crazy as I thought you were!)
>
> » **You misunderstood me.** (I'm not as bad as you think.)
>
> » **That's just who I am.** (I'm a sinner, so that excuses my behavior.)
>
> » **I made a mistake.** (Don't we all?)
>
> » **I didn't mean to do it.** (I didn't mean to get caught.)
>
> » **I'm having a bad day.** (I deserve better.)

Which of the excuses listed above can you identify with?

What is a recent example (or a typical situation) when you used one of these excuses instead of truly being broken and repentant over your sin?

As a group, describe what true repentance would look like in these cases, using the steps below.

STEP 1: Acknowledge that you have sinned against God.

STEP 2: Confess forms of false repentance and selfish regret (remorse, resolution, etc.).

STEP 3: Discern and repent of the underlying heart motivations that drive you to this sin.

STEP 4: Receive God's forgiveness by faith.

STEP 5: Rely upon God's power to turn away from sin.

Repeat this process, working through as many responses as time allows: identify excuses, share examples, and practice true repentance.

HEART IDOLATRY 6

BIG IDEA

We've said that the Christian walk consists of two repeated steps: repentance and faith. In Lesson Five, we dealt with repentance. Now we turn our attention to the topic of faith. Remember, we grow through believing the gospel. That's the emphasis of this week's discussion and exercise. Easy enough, right? This week's goal is to take "believing the gospel" out of the abstract and make it concrete.

NOTES:

lesson

ARTICLE

6 HEART IDOLATRY

Over the past few weeks, we have said that repentance and faith should be the continual, consistent pattern of the Christian life. Last week we examined the nature of true repentance. This week we want to dive deeper into the subject of faith.

Think for a moment about this question: what one thing should I do to grow more as a Christian? If someone asked you that question, how would you respond? Would you suggest some basic spiritual discipline, such as reading the Bible, praying, finding Christian friends, repenting of sin, or learning theology?

The crowds brought this exact query to Jesus in John 6. His answer may surprise you:

> *Then they asked him, "What must we do to do the works God requires?" Jesus answered, "The work of God is this: to believe in the one he has sent." (John 6:28–29)*

Notice that they are asking Jesus what they must do to live a life that pleases God. Jesus answers that the *work* of God is to *believe*. In other words, the Christian life is not about doing, it is about believing. Getting this right is crucial to sanctification. Most of us are naturally "doers." We gladly embrace the next project, the next challenge, the next assignment. So our pursuit of Christian maturity produces a lot of busy effort, but little lasting change. Why is this so? *Because we are doing too much and believing too little.*

You see, our **surface sins** are only symptoms of a deeper problem. Underneath every external sin is a **heart idol**—a false god that has eclipsed the true God in our thoughts or affections. To paraphrase Martin Luther, every sin is in some way a breaking of the first commandment ("You shall have no other gods before me"). Luther wrote, "As [the First] Commandment is the very first, highest and best, from which all the others proceed…so also its work, that is, faith or confidence in God's favor at all times, is the very first, highest and best, from which all other [works] must proceed, exist, remain, be directed and measured."* In other words, keeping God primary is foundational to spiritual growth. The key to gospel-driven transformation is learning to repent of the "sin beneath the sin"—the deeply rooted idolatry and unbelief that drive our more visible sins.

As a case study, let's take the surface sin of gossip—talking about people behind their backs in judgmental or destructive ways. Why do we gossip? What are we looking for that we should be finding in God?

Here are some common heart idols that can manifest themselves in the surface sin of gossip:

> » **The idol of approval** (I want the approval of the people I'm talking to)
>
> » **The idol of control** (Using gossip as a way to manipulate/control others)
>
> » **The idol of reputation** (I want to feel important, so I cut someone else down verbally)
>
> » **The idol of success** (Someone is succeeding—and I'm not—so I gossip about him)
>
> » **The idol of security** (Talking about others masks my own insecurity)
>
> » **The idol of pleasure** (Someone else is enjoying life—and I'm not—so I attack her)
>
> » **The idol of knowledge** (Talking about people is a way of showing I know more)
>
> » **The idol of recognition** (Talking about others gets people to notice me)
>
> » **The idol of respect** (That person disrespected me, so I'm going to disrespect him)

---

* Martin Luther, *Treatise on Good Works*, section 9, (1520).

All these idols are false saviors promoting false gospels. Every one of these things—approval, control, reputation, success, security, pleasure, knowledge, recognition, respect—is something we already have in Jesus because of the gospel! But when we are not living in light of the gospel, we turn to these idols to give us what only Jesus can truly give us.

Another way to identify your particular heart idols is to ask *what do I love, trust, or fear?* For example, if I fear being single, "being in a relationship" will probably be my idol (because it promises to deliver me from the "hell" of singleness). If I trust "having enough," security will probably be my idol (because it promises that I'll never be without anything). If I love order and structure, control will probably be my idol (because if I'm in charge, I can make sure things are in order).

Reflecting on the "sin beneath our sin" shows why the gospel is essential for true heart change. It's possible to repent of surface sins for a lifetime yet never address the deeper heart issues behind them! At the moment I sin, I have already broken the first commandment. An idol has taken God's place in my soul. I am trusting in that idol, rather than in God, to be my Savior. I need to apply the gospel by (1) *repenting* of my deep heart idolatry and (2) *believing*—that is, turning my mind toward the specific gospel promises that break the power of my characteristic idols.

According to Dr. Steve Childers, faith "involves learning how to set the affections of our mind and heart on Christ…. Faith requires a continual rehearsing and delighting in the many privileges that are now ours *in* Christ."** Notice the two aspects of faith: setting our affections on Christ and delighting in the privileges that are ours in Christ. I must worship Jesus (not my idols), and I must remind myself of what is really true about me because of Jesus.

Let's go back again to our example of gossip. Let's imagine that I have identified *respect* as the dominant idol that drives me to gossip. After I acknowledge my sin and repent of it, I exercise faith in two ways. First, I pause and worship Jesus because he laid aside his right to be respected,

---

** Steven L. Childers, "True Spirituality: The Transforming Power of the Gospel," available at www.gca.cc.

becoming humbled to the point of death (Phil. 2:5–11). Second, I remind myself of the gospel truth that I no longer need to crave the respect of others because I have the approval of God through faith in Jesus (2 Cor. 5:17–21). Whether people respect me or not is immaterial: God's grace has freed me from demanding my own respect, and now I live for the fame and honor of Jesus (1 Cor. 10:31).

This exercise is fairly simple in the abstract, but it can be much more difficult when thinking through your own personal patterns of sin. So set aside some intentional time to (1) identify your common surface sins and (2) prayerfully consider what heart idols might lie behind them. Then (3) worship Jesus for his victory over that idol and (4) find specific gospel promises you can rely on to help defeat the power of that idol. Be sure to invite others into your process of reflection and repentance. As one writer has put it, "You can't see your own face." We need each other in order to see our sin clearly and deal with it honestly.

As you learn to live a gospel-centered life, remember that this is the essence of walking with Jesus. Repentance and faith are not steps *on* the path; they *are* the path. The work of God is to *believe*.

MISSION

BIG IDEA

The gospel is simultaneously at work in us and through us. Inwardly, our desires and motives are being changed as we repent and believe the gospel. As we experience Christ's love in this way, we are compelled to engage those around us with the same kind of redemptive love. God's grace brings renewal everywhere, in us and through us.

NOTES:

7

THE GOSPEL PROPELS US OUTWARD

For you were called to freedom, brothers. Only do not use your freedom as an opportunity for the flesh, but through love serve one another. (Gal. 5:13 ESV)

When we truly understand the depth and richness of the gospel, we naturally feel joy, delight, and freedom because of who Jesus is and what he has done for us. But as this verse teaches, it's possible to use even our freedom as "an opportunity for the flesh." Our sinful hearts can take the good benefits of the gospel and use them for selfish purposes.

Nowhere is this more evident than in our tendency to make the gospel a private reality. When we hear words like *transformation, renewal,* or *growth,* we conceive of those benefits as being primarily personal and internal—*my* transformation, *my* growth, the gospel's renewal of *my* heart. And the gospel *is* personal and internal. But it's also much more than that. When God's grace is working *on* us and *in* us, it will also work itself out *through* us. The internal renewal of our minds and hearts creates an external propulsion that moves us out in love and service to others. The following diagram is helpful in illustrating this concept.

God's grace is the driving force of all change. The chart reminds us that God's grace has both an inward and an outward movement that mirror each other. Internally, the grace of God moves me to see my sin, respond in repentance and faith, and then experience the joy of transformation. Externally, the grace of God moves me to see opportunities for love and service, respond in repentance and faith, and experience joy as I see God work through me.

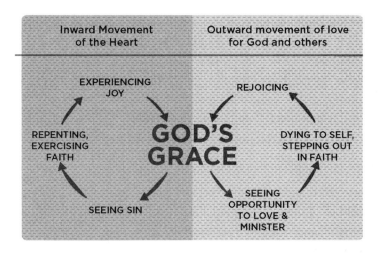

In other words, the gospel is not just the answer to your internal sins, struggles, and heart idols. It is also the answer to your failure to love others, engage the culture, and live missionally. If the gospel is renewing you internally, it will also be propelling you externally. It must do so, for it is "the good news of the kingdom" (Matt. 9:35), and the kingdom of God is not personal and private! Jesus taught us to pray, "Your kingdom come, your will be done, on earth as it is in heaven" (Matt. 6:10). When we pray for the coming of God's kingdom, we are praying both that Jesus would reign in the hearts of people (internal) and that his will would be done everywhere just as it is in heaven (external).

What does this external movement of the gospel look like in practice? Let me give an example. I know that I should love my neighbors. Jesus commanded it. In fact, he said it was the fulfillment of the law (Gal. 5:14). But my next-door neighbor and I just don't have a lot in common. He is much older and has different tastes in everything—music, movies, food, cars, lifestyle. While I enjoy talking about a new musician I've discovered or a good book I've read recently, he'd rather reminisce about the old days when he served with the Marines in Vietnam.

For months I labored under guilt in my relationship with my neighbor. I knew I *should* reach out and befriend him. But that sense of "should" had no motivational power. It was law, not gospel. It could show me what I ought to be doing, but it could not change my heart so that I actually wanted to do it. I was faced with a dilemma: either force myself to love and serve my neighbor even though I didn't *want* to, or ignore him and do nothing at all. I knew that ignoring him was sin, but the first option didn't feel much better. Was joyless, mechanical obedience really honoring to Jesus? Did God intend his commands to feel like drudgery?

When faced with this dilemma, most people settle for either legalism (obey even though you don't feel like it) or license (don't obey at all). But neither of these is the gospel! The gospel of God's grace is the fuel for mission, and when we run low on that fuel, our love and service to others grinds to a halt.

The answer to my dilemma with my neighbor came through the gospel. As God's grace began to renew my heart, I saw that the root problem was my own selfishness and lack of love. My love for my neighbor was conditional—if he were younger, or smarter, or had more in common with me, I would have appreciated him more. I began to repent of this sin and renew my mind by the promises of the gospel—especially the fact that God loved *me* while I was still a sinner (Rom. 5:8). God had graciously moved toward me when I had nothing in common with him. Certainly, by God's grace, I could love my neighbor in the same way! As the gospel renewed my heart, a strange thing happened. My attitude toward my neighbor began to change. I began to feel a true love and appreciation for him. And it wasn't a feeling I had mustered up, but one that came naturally. The internal renewal of the gospel propelled me outward in love and service toward my neighbor. Mission became a joy, not a burden.

Grasping the external propulsion of God's grace is crucial to our understanding of mission. It means that mission is not a duty (something we "should do") but a natural overflow of the gospel's work inside us. If you aren't motivated to love, serve, and speak the gospel to people, the answer isn't to "just do it." The answer is to examine your heart, repent of sin, and discern where your unbelief is short-circuiting the natural outward movement of the gospel. As the gospel renews your heart, it will also renew your desire to move out in faith into the relationships and opportunities God places in your path.

To put it simply, the grace of God is always going somewhere—moving forward, extending his kingdom, propelling his people toward love and service to others. As we learn to live in light of the gospel, mission should be the natural overflow. God's grace brings renewal internally (in us) so that it might bring renewal externally (through us).

7

EXERCISE GETTING TO THE HEART OF MISSION

EXAMINING YOUR HEART FOR MISSION

1. Identify a missional opportunity in your life in which you are not motivated to do what you "should" do. Here are some categories to jump-start your thinking: showing hospitality to neighbors; actively praying for and engaging with co-workers; sharing the gospel with a family member; serving someone in poverty; giving generously; leading spiritually as a spouse or parent; defending the biblical worldview on a particular issue.

2. What heart issues hinder you from rightly motivated action in this situation? As you pray and reflect on the root of your inactivity, what do you discern? Be as specific and thorough as you can about the things that keep you from expressing gospel-centered love toward others.

3. Repentance: What sin do you see in yourself that you need to repent of? **Faith:** What specific gospel promises or truths are you not really believing?

FORGIVENESS

BIG IDEA

The gospel that works in us always works through us. It shows its power in our relationships and actions. One key way this happens is when we forgive others biblically.

NOTES:

THE GOSPEL EMPOWERS US TO FORGIVE

Forgiving people who harm us is one of the most difficult things to do in life. And the deeper the wound, the more challenging it gets. We often feel confused about what real forgiveness looks like. Are we to "forgive and forget"? Is that even possible? And what exactly does it mean to "love my enemy"? What about the person who sexually abused me? Or the boss who furthered his career at my expense? Or the spouse who cheated on me? Or the friend who slandered me and damaged my reputation?

We have seen that when the gospel really takes root *in* us, it begins to work itself out *through* us. Forgiveness is one area where the gospel must "go to work" in our lives. In fact, forgiving others really isn't possible unless we are living in light of God's forgiveness ourselves. So let's consider how the gospel moves us toward forgiveness.

The gospel begins with God's movement toward us. God takes the initiative, though he is the offended party. He acted to reconcile the relationship "while we were God's enemies" (Rom. 5:10). Our sin had separated us from him (Isa. 59:2). He had every right to condemn us, to resist us, and to sever the relationship, but he did not. Instead, he moved toward us: "While we were still sinners, Christ died for us" (Rom. 5:8).

However, reconciliation with God requires our repentance. By forgiving our sin, God extends the *offer* of reconciliation, but reconciliation is not complete until we repent and receive his forgiveness by faith. Notice how both dynamics are reflected in 2 Corinthians 5:19–20: "God was reconciling the world to himself in Christ, not counting men's sins against them. And he has committed to us the message of reconciliation. We are therefore Christ's ambassadors, as though God were making his appeal through us. We implore you on Christ's behalf: Be reconciled to God."

Scripture gives all credit, glory, and praise to God for our salvation, because it is only by his gracious initiative that we are able to respond (Eph. 2:8–9). But our response of repentance and faith is essential. Salvation is not universal. Only those who repent and receive God's gracious offer will be reconciled to him.

So we might summarize God's forgiveness this way: By moving toward us, God invites and enables us to move toward him. The gospel starts with God (the offended party) moving toward us (the offenders). He cancels our debt and opens to us an opportunity for reconciliation. If we acknowledge our sin and repent, we are reconciled to God and able to experience the joy and delight of relationship with him.

What, then, does it look like for us to forgive others as God has forgiven us? This, after all, is what the Bible commands: "Be kind to one another, tenderhearted, forgiving one another, just as God in Christ forgave you" (Eph. 4:32 ESV). Scripture assumes that if we have truly experienced God's forgiveness in the gospel, we will be radically forgiving toward others. By contrast, if we are unforgiving, resentful, or bitter toward others, it is a sure sign that we are not living out of the deep joy and freedom of the gospel.

Our forgiveness of others is intended to mirror the forgiveness God has given us. We are to take the initiative: "If you are offering your gift at the altar and there remember that your brother has something against you, leave your gift there before the altar and go. First be reconciled to your brother, and then come and offer your gift" (Matt. 5:23–24 ESV). We are to offer forgiveness and open a door for reconciliation. But reconciliation is always contingent upon the other person's repentance. Christian author and counselor Dan Allender has suggested a helpful analogy: "Forgiveness involves a heart that cancels the debt but does not lend new money until repentance occurs."* Like God, we take the initiative to move toward those who have offended us and we invite them to move toward us in repentance.

What this means is that our work is not done once we have forgiven someone. Our heart's desire is not simply to forgive the offense but ultimately to see the other person reconciled to God and to us. We want to see sin's power over this person destroyed. We cannot make this happen, but we are to pray for it, long for it, and welcome it. Where do we find the power to do this? After all, it's hard enough just *forgiving* someone who has deeply wounded us. How do we find the grace and strength to long for restoration?

The answer, of course, is the gospel. The gospel doesn't just show us *how* to forgive; it *empowers* us to forgive.

When we say, "I just can't forgive that person for what he did to me," we are essentially saying, "That person's sin is greater than mine." Our awareness of our own sin is very small, while our awareness of another's sin is very big. Our underlying feeling is that *we* deserve to be forgiven but the person who offended us does not. We are living with a small view of God's holiness, a small view of our own sin, and a small view of the cross of Jesus.

But when we embrace a gospel perspective on our own sin, we recognize that the sin debt God has forgiven on our behalf is greater than any sin that has been committed against us. And as we grow in our awareness of God's holiness, we begin to see more clearly the distance between his perfection and our imperfection. As the significance of Jesus' work on the cross grows in our consciousness, our willingness and ability to seek restoration with others will also grow. After all, if God forgave the massive offense of our sin against him, how could we not forgive the sin of others—which, though it may be severe, pales in comparison with our own guilt before a holy and righteous God?

---

* Dr. Dan B. Allender and Dr. Tremper Longman III, *Bold Love* (Colorado Springs: NavPress, 1992), p. 162.

Forgiveness is costly. It means canceling a debt when we feel we have every right to demand payment. It means absorbing the pain, hurt, shame, and grief of someone's sin against us. It means longing for repentance and restoration. But this is exactly how God has acted toward us in Jesus Christ. And through the gospel, the Holy Spirit empowers us to do the same toward others.

GETTING TO THE HEART OF FORGIVENESS

HOMEWORK

(Answer these questions before your meeting. You may need a separate sheet of paper.)

1. Think of one or two people you need to forgive (or forgive more deeply). If you have a hard time thinking of someone, ask God to reveal someone to you. Here are some scenarios and feelings that might bring someone to mind: someone you have distanced yourself from; people you feel uncomfortable around; people you no longer enjoy; relational conflicts you keep rehearsing in your mind; someone who said or did something that hurt you; feelings of anger, bitterness, irritation, fear, gossip, or a critical spirit.

Write down one or two people who come to mind.

2. What irritates or disturbs you most about this person?

3. What issues of "justice" are involved in the situation? How has this person wronged you, hurt you, or sinned against you?

4. What conditions do you instinctively want to place on this person before you truly forgive him or her? In others words, what does your heart want to require from this person before you release him or her? What specifically would you desire the person to say or do?

5. Describe your own debt before God. How is it far greater than the debt of the people you have listed (yet it is cancelled and forgiven)? Do not rush through this question. Take time to describe your indebtedness in terms of the specific ways sin manifests itself in your life.

6. How has your previous way of relating to these people reflected a small view of your own debt and a small view of Christ's forgiveness?

CONFLICT

BIG IDEA

Conflict is something we all experience (regularly), but often handle in very fleshly ways. The gospel gives us a pattern and a means to healthy conflict resolution.

NOTES:

lesson

ARTICLE

THE GOSPEL HELPS US FIGHT FAIRLY

We have seen that as the gospel renews us internally, it also flows out of us to bring renewal to our relationships. Nothing is more common to relationships than conflict. If the gospel is not affecting the way we deal with conflict, then it's probably not touching us very deeply! In this article, we will consider how the gospel helps us fight fairly.

Think of the most recent fight you've had. Perhaps the conflict was with your spouse, a family member, or a work associate. Now, set aside the circumstances of the argument (what the issue was, how it made you feel, who was right or wrong) and take a moment to ponder your actions during the conflict. Your behavior probably falls into one of two categories.

Some people are **attackers**. They like to be on the offensive. They place a high value on justice, so it matters greatly to them who is right and who is wrong. Below are signs that you might be an attacker.

- » You deal with anger or frustration by "venting" it.
- » You argue your case passionately.
- » You ask questions like "How do you know?" and "Can you prove that?"
- » You want to fight until the fight is over.
- » You cross-examine like a lawyer in order to "get to the heart of the conflict."
- » Winning the argument is more important than loving the opponent.
- » You turn the argument to focus on the other person, even if it began with you as the focal point.

On the other end of the spectrum are **withdrawers**. People with this tendency often find themselves on the defensive. They tend to avoid or ignore conflict and, when pressed into an argument, they respond in sullen silence or apathetic passivity. If you're a withdrawer, here are some patterns you might recognize:

» You deal with anger or frustration by suppressing it.

» You have opinions but keep them to yourself in order to "keep the peace."

» You ask questions like, do we have to talk about this now? and does it matter?

» You'd rather avoid a fight than win one.

» You sometimes physically leave an argument in order to "get some space."

These are typical ways we respond to disagreement, frustration, offense, or hurt. The fact that these responses are considered "normal" (i.e. natural) is a clue that they may not be biblical (i.e. supernatural).

How, then, do we move toward resolving conflict in a biblical manner? Let's learn from the disagreement between Paul and Peter in Galatians 2. This quarrel arose as the early church was expanding beyond Jerusalem and many Gentiles were being converted to faith in Jesus. The Jewish Christians imported some of their traditional practices into their worship of Jesus. The Gentiles, on the other hand, had no allegiance to Jewish customs like circumcision or dietary regulations.

Peter, a Jew, understood the gospel well enough to embrace the new Gentile believers with no strings attached (Acts 10:9–48). But his application of the gospel got tested when he found himself in mixed company. Some legalistic Jewish teachers from Jerusalem had begun to impose Jewish customs and laws on Gentile converts. When these teachers came to Antioch, where Peter was fellowshipping and eating with Gentiles, Peter began to separate himself from the Gentiles.

Peter's attempt to appease the legalistic Jews compounded the problem because it implied that he agreed with their beliefs. Eventually, even Barnabas followed suit. The two men had fallen into hypocrisy, professing to be one with the Gentiles in Christ, yet acting in ways that destroyed that unity.

As he observed this behavior, Paul knew he could not ignore or withdraw from the situation. The stakes were too high. But he also had to approach it in the right way. "Flying off the handle" wasn't going to bring about the kind of reconciliation he wanted. Though this passage does not give all the details, its description of Paul's interaction with Peter is a good example of a gospel-centered approach to conflict.

> But when Cephas [Peter] came to Antioch, I [Paul] opposed him to his face, because he stood condemned. For before certain men came from James, he was eating with the Gentiles; but when they came he drew back and separated himself, fearing the circumcision party. And the rest of the Jews acted hypocritically along with him, so that even Barnabas was led astray by their hypocrisy. But when I saw that their conduct was not in step with the truth of the gospel, I said to [Peter] before them all, "If you, though a Jew, live like a Gentile and not like a Jew, how can you force the Gentiles to live like Jews?" (Gal. 2:11–14 ESV)

Note these aspects of Paul's actions:

PAUL APPROACHED PETER PUBLICLY. He didn't avoid Peter, gossip about him, or try to bully him. He confronted him, going directly to the person with whom he had the conflict. In this case the confrontation was public. This isn't always necessary, but since the sin was public and had far-reaching consequences, Paul made sure the confrontation fit the situation.

PAUL'S MOTIVATION WAS NOT SELF-DEFENSE OR SELF-INTEREST BUT THE DEFENSE OF THE GOSPEL. "Their conduct was not in step with the truth of the gospel" (Gal. 2:14). Paul's concern for the gospel and relationships in the church body outweighed the temptation to either attack or withdraw.

PAUL PRESENTED THE ISSUE PLAINLY AND INVITED A RESPONSE FROM PETER. "If you, though a Jew, live like a Gentile and not like a Jew, how can you force the Gentiles to live like Jews?" (Gal. 2:14).

This sort of gospel-centered confrontation mirrors God's movement toward us in the gospel. God did not pour out his wrath on us (attack) or remove his presence from us (withdraw). Instead, he sacrificially moved toward us in the person of Jesus, full of grace and truth. Jesus confronted sin, invited relationship, and provided a way of reconciliation. Thus, the gospel provides the pattern of biblical conflict resolution. We have a proper motivation (love), confidence (faith), and means for resolving conflict (grace and truth).

The gospel calls us to repent of our sinful patterns of attacking and withdrawing. And the gospel empowers us to move into conflict by faith, with a humble, confident, God-glorifying intentionality. We can forsake the "normal" way of doing things for the gospel way.

EXERCISE 9

GOSPEL-CENTERED CONFLICT RESOLUTION

The chart below outlines the differences between attacking and withdrawing and contrasts them with a gospel-centered approach to conflict. Not everything in this chart is going to resonate with every person or conflict, so focus on whichever descriptions are particularly relevant to you. The goal is to help you identify what is at the root of the unhealthy patterns of conflict in your life and to provide a clear path toward gospel resolution.

ASPECT	ATTACKING	WITH-DRAWING	GOSPEL
HEART FOUNDATION	Self-righteousness	Insecurity	Repentance, forgiveness
POWER SOURCE	Flesh, pride	Flesh, fear	The Holy Spirit
COMMITMENT	To be right	To avoid conflict	To understand & engage
DIRECTION	To argue or subdue	To deny or appease	To convey & invite
FEELING	Life is safe	Life is less painful	Life is challenging
GOAL	Self-protection	"Peace"	God's glory, their good
RESULT	Hurt, divisiveness	Bitterness, separation	Healing, reconciliation

How do you usually deal with conflict; do you tend toward attacking or withdrawing? Which descriptions above do you particularly identify with?

A GOSPEL-CENTERED APPROACH TO CONFLICT

Outlined below is a process of dealing with conflict in a gospel-centered manner. Each aspect is listed, along with some questions that will help you assess your tendencies in that area. You may call to mind past experiences or even a current conflict with someone. Remember, the goal is to recognize unhealthy patterns in your life and to practice applying the gospel more effectively.

1. HEART FOUNDATION: Identify your tendency toward either self-righteousness or insecurity. Do you tend to be defensive, or blame others, or always think you are right (self-righteousness)? Do you tend to harbor anger or gossip, or stuff things to avoid confrontation (insecurity)? Confess these things as sin, to God and those involved.

2. POWER SOURCE: Acknowledge what drives your attacking or withdrawing. Are you concerned with losing face, being wrong, disrupting the peace, other's disapproval, etc? By faith, affirm your trust in the power of the Holy Spirit to free you from these sins of pride and fear.

3. COMMITMENT: Communicate to those involved that you want to seek resolution. To help with this, identify what else you tend to seek instead of resolution (being right, being "safe", comfort)? Reject these pursuits as false and destructive.

4. DIRECTION: As you engage the person you are having conflict with, talk honestly and respectfully about your thoughts and feelings, and invite the other party to do the same. Do you understand each other? What usually gets in the way of your understanding, or being understood (anger, argumentativeness, dishonesty, timidity, assumptions you make about others, etc.)?

5. FEELING AND GOAL: Talk about what it will cost each of you to resolve this conflict. Specify what steps need to be taken toward resolution. Pray for God's will to be done (his glory and each other's good). Ask him to enable you to pay the price of resolution, thanking him for paying the ultimate price of death to resolve the ultimate conflict of our sinful rebellion.

LEADER'S NOTES

FROM THE AUTHORS

God gave us the privilege of planting a wonderfully messy church, where mature Christians, newer Christians, and lots of non-Christians and skeptics are all mixed up together. Our church is structured around these groups called missional communities, which are kind of like traditional church small groups, only completely different.

The ideal missional community consists of a small band of Christians living on mission together, and inviting their non-Christian friends to join in conversation and interaction about the gospel of Jesus. This seemed like a really great idea...until we started doing it. We quickly discovered two significant problems:

1. Most traditional "church small group" material was written for a Christian audience, and therefore non-Christians relate to it about as well as a cattle rancher relates to vegetarians.

2. Many Christians have a weak and anemic understanding of the gospel, so asking them to talk about how the gospel is transforming them is like asking a teenage boy band to talk about the finer elements of Mozart's work.

So we wrote The Gospel-Centered Life *in order to shape "gospel DNA" in our church in a way that was accessible to both Christians and non-Christians.*

The Gospel-Centered Life *is intended to help Christians understand how the gospel shapes every aspect of life and conduct. Colossians 1:6 says that the gospel is "continually bearing fruit and increasing" in and among us, even after we first believe it. How does that happen? Why is a continual rediscovery and application of the gospel so important? How will our personal growth and missional life be stunted if we don't grasp the gospel deeply? These are the questions that GCL seeks to answer.*

ABOUT THIS STUDY

The biggest advantage to *The Gospel-Centered Life* is its flexibility. It's appropriate for missional church-planting contexts, established churches, and parachurch or campus ministries. It creates good dialogue among groups of mature Christians as well as among new Christians and non-Christians. This Leader's Guide contains all the information needed to facilitate the group, so it can be led by an experienced small group leader or by a high school student. And because the concepts are basic and biblical, it adapts easily to different cultural settings (it's already been used with international students, African refugees, and Chinese house-churches).

THE GOSPEL-CENTERED LIFE IS IDEAL FOR:

- » Pastors and leaders who want to spur gospel renewal in their churches and ministries

- » Church-planters who want to form gospel DNA in the churches they start

- » Students and campus ministers who are looking to live out the gospel on campus

- » Christians who want to be more deeply formed around the gospel

- » Small group leaders who are looking for content that "works" with diverse groups of people

- » Missionaries who are looking for simple material to disciple new Christians

THE GOSPEL GRID

BIG IDEA

If the gospel is constantly "bearing fruit and growing" (Col. 1:6), then everything has to do with the gospel—God, humanity, salvation, worship, relationships, shopping, recreation, work, personality…everything! The objective in this lesson is to establish a framework for talking about the gospel. This framework will get worked out in greater detail over the next two sessions, so this lesson is designed to help us understand the concepts and begin exploring how they relate to actual life.

LESSON OVERVIEW

I. BIBLE CONVERSATION	Read and talk about the passage(s) [10 min]
II. ARTICLE	Read *The Gospel Grid* together [10 min]
III. DISCUSSION	Process concepts together [15 min]
IV. EXERCISE	Apply the concepts using a specific exercise [15 min]
V. WRAP-UP	Final thoughts and prayer [5 min]

BIBLE CONVERSATION *10 minutes*

We are focusing on two major concepts in this lesson: God's holiness and our sinfulness. The passages highlight these concepts. The goal here is not to say everything there is to say about these ideas. The goal is simply to get the conversation going in a way that establishes a biblical foundation for the concepts, which will unfold throughout the discussion.

`SETUP`   We are basically going to talk about two concepts: how we view God and how we view ourselves. When it comes to the way we view God, there tends to be a spectrum of opinion. At one end, some people have a very high view of God, to the point that he is so totally "other" that he is uninvolved in our daily lives. At the other end, some people have a very personal view of God, to the point that he is so much like a best friend that his holiness is neglected. The same is true for the way we view ourselves: the spectrum ranges from the idea that people are basically good to the idea that people are basically bad. Let's see how we land on each of these questions.

`ASK`   Which end of the spectrum do you lean toward when it comes to God: is he majestic and somewhat removed, or so personal that you don't really think much about his holiness?

`ASK`   Which thought best represents your view of people: basically good or basically bad?

Let's look at two Bible passages that highlight these two concepts. The main two questions to ask as we read these verses are (1) "What does this say about God?" and (2) "What does this say about me?"

`READ`   The first passage is Isaiah 55:6–9. (Have someone read Isaiah 55:6–9 out loud.)

`ASK`   What is your initial reaction to this passage? What stands out to you?

What does this say about God—and us?

`READ`   The next passage is Jeremiah 17:9–10. (Have someone read Jeremiah 17:9–10 out loud.)

`ASK`   What is your initial reaction to this passage? What stands out to you?

What does this say about God—and us?

`TRANSITION TO ARTICLE`   These passages introduce us to the biblical view of God's holiness and our sinfulness. To get a more focused understanding of these ideas, let's read this article together. We are going to read it aloud, taking turns at the paragraph breaks. Then I have some discussion questions that will help us process it together.

ARTICLE *10 minutes*

This lesson assumes a basic familiarity with the gospel. If that's a generous assumption for your group, consider reading through the "Gospel Overview" in the Front Matter together before you progress through the reading for this lesson. It will add about 10 minutes to your study, but it will be well worth it.

The point of reading an article together is twofold: (1) To explain key concepts so everyone in your group has a common understanding and language, and (2) to provide a focus for conversation. Remember, we are trying to help your group learn how to talk about the gospel in relation to their actual lives. In many cases, people do not talk about the gospel or their lives because they simply don't have much to say. The article gives them content to talk about.

Ask your group to turn to the article *The Gospel Grid* in their Participant's Guide and read it aloud together, taking turns at the paragraph breaks.

TRANSITION TO DISCUSSION   There is some good stuff here. Let's talk about this article. As we do, I want to focus on understanding the concepts and relating them to our lives. If there is something you don't get, by all means ask questions so we can talk it through together. As we go, I will try to ask questions that will help us apply this to our lives.

DISCUSSION *15 minutes*

These questions are aimed at helping the group talk through the Cross Chart. Those who do not understand it will be able to work it out in community, and those who "get it" will benefit from learning how to articulate it. You may want to ask follow-up questions as you go.

1. Let's recap the main ideas from the article.

ASK   What are the implications of viewing the gospel only as the "entry point" to the Christian life?

`ASK`   What two things are to be growing as we mature in faith?

`ASK`   What are the two ways we "shrink the cross"?

2. Let's personalize these concepts a bit.

`ASK`   How have you seen your view of God change and grow in the past year (top line of chart)? How did this happen?

Sometimes it is hard to identify the ways we minimize and justify our sin (bottom line of the chart). Take a look at the supplement *Six Ways of Minimizing Sin* in your Participant's Guide. Let's read through these together and then talk about how we relate to these descriptions.

`ASK`   Which one of these do you see yourself doing most often? (Ask everyone to share the one they relate to the most.)

`ASK`   Can anyone share a recent example of a time when you minimized or justified your sin in one of these ways?

`TRANSITION TO EXERCISE`   This is really good. We are talking about some significant concepts that we will continue to explore in the next two sessions. I want to end with an exercise that will help us apply what we have been talking about to a specific area we all deal with. *Hand out copies of the exercise—Judging Others—to everyone in the group.*

EXERCISE *15 minutes*

The point of this exercise is to apply the Cross Chart to a specific issue that will help everyone see (1) how their sin is rooted in a small view of the gospel and (2) how a big view of the gospel helps us overcome sin. **Note:** *Not everyone needs to answer every question aloud, but try to draw out as many people as you can throughout the exercise.*

`SETUP`   Let's take the issue of judging others. We all do this in various ways. So let's start by quickly brainstorming a list of ways we judge others. Even if it's just the little everyday judgments we make, what are some specific ways we judge others?

Write down a list of ways we judge others based on the group's answers.

So that's how we judge others. Let's talk about why we do this.

ASK　What are the reasons we judge others? Let's brainstorm another list together.

ASK　How do these reasons reflect a small view of God's holiness?

ASK　How do these reasons reflect a small view of our own sin?

Okay, let's get personal. Think of a specific person in your life that you are often judgmental toward.

ASK　How would a bigger view of God's holiness affect that relationship?

ASK　How would a bigger view of your sin affect that relationship?

TRANSITION TO WRAP-UP　This has been really good. Thanks for sharing. We are going to continue working through these concepts over the next two weeks. Before we wrap up, does anyone have any lingering questions or comments?...Okay, let's spend a few minutes praying together. If some of you want to pray, I will close in a few minutes.

WRAP-UP *5 minutes*

Questions, comments, prayer.

PRETENDING & PERFORMING

BIG IDEA

This lesson deals with how we "shrink the cross," which is to say that something is lacking in our understanding, appreciation, or application of Jesus' sacrifice for our sin. This manifests itself in two main ways: **pretending** and **performing**. Pretending minimizes sin by making ourselves out to be something we are not. Performing minimizes God's holiness by reducing his standard to something we can meet, thereby meriting his favor. Both are rooted in an inadequate view of God's holiness and our identity.

LESSON OVERVIEW

I. BIBLE CONVERSATION	Read and talk about the passage(s) [10 min]
II. ARTICLE	Read *Shrinking the Cross* together [10 min]
III. DISCUSSION	Process concepts together [15 min]
IV. EXERCISE	Apply the concepts using a specific exercise [15 min]
V. WRAP-UP	Final thoughts and prayer [5 min]

BIBLE CONVERSATION *10 minutes*

Each of these passages illustrates a false righteousness. First, a self-righteous Pharisee can see the sin of others but not his own. Then a young man seeks to get eternal life by keeping the law. These may be familiar stories to some, so you will have to work at getting people to read them honestly.

SETUP We are going to read two stories in Luke 18 (really, a parable and a story). Let's read the parable first. It is pretty straightforward, so let's read it and then answer a few questions about it.

READ The parable is in Luke 18:9–14. (Have someone read Luke 18:9–14 aloud.)

ASK As we read, which character did you identify with? Which point of view did you take as being most like yours? Why?

ASK What do you like/dislike about the idea of being like the Pharisee?

ASK What do you like/dislike about the idea of being like the tax collector?

ASK Why is the Pharisee the "bad guy" in this parable? The stuff he is doing isn't bad!

READ The story begins in verse 18. (Have someone read Luke 18:18–23 aloud.)

ASK How would you describe this man's view of God?

ASK How would you describe his view of himself?

TRANSITION TO ARTICLE These two passages reveal our tendency to think more highly of ourselves than we should, and to think less of God than we should. The article we are going to read calls these tendencies pretending and performing. Let's read it together and then we can process how and why this happens.

ARTICLE *10 minutes*

Some people feel that reading an article feels too formal. We agree, but we have also seen the benefit of getting everyone on the same page with a common language. The content in the article acts as kindling to get the conversation going. Without it, you will get a bunch of smoke.

Ask your group to turn to the article *Shrinking the Cross* in their Participant's Guide and read it aloud together, taking turns at the paragraph breaks.

DISCUSSION *15 minutes*

1. Let's talk about the top line of the chart first.

`ASK` Do you ever have the feeling that you don't want to know God's commands because of what the implications might be?

`ASK` Does thinking about God's holiness tend to move you to worship or to fear?

`ASK` How would you respond to the other question in the article: "As God thinks of you right now, what is the look on his face?" Why is that your response? What do you think the various responses say about our views of God?

2. Let's talk about the bottom line of the chart now.

`ASK` How do you feel about seeing the depths of your brokenness, or being seen by others in this way? Are you hesitant or willing? Why?

`ASK` Do you like to be convicted of your sin or does it feel like a "crushing weight"?

`ASK` How would you respond to the question in the article: "What do you count on to give you a sense of 'personal credibility' (validity, acceptance, good standing)?"

`ASK` Looking at the types of righteousness described in the article, which one do you identify with most? Why? How has that played out with people in your life?

`TRANSITION TO EXERCISE` It is eye-opening to see how prevalent these tendencies are in all of us, and this probably only scratches the surface! We will continue to talk about these concepts as we move forward. As always, I think it is important to try to work out these concepts practically, so I have an exercise that will help us do that.

EXERCISE: Right and Wrong *15 minutes*

1. Turn to the *Right and Wrong* exercise with your group.

2. Read aloud the paragraph at the top. Then give people a few minutes to answer the questions individually.

`ASK` What are some of the rules you wrote down?

`ASK` How do these morally neutral rules become moral issues in our minds?

`ASK` Why do you think we have such a strong desire to be right?

`ASK` How do our rules shrink the cross and keep us from seeing our sin?

`ASK` What practical difference would it make to get your sense of righteousness from Jesus instead of from your rules?

`ASK` Can you think of someone who imposes his or her rules on you? How do you usually relate to that person? Do you feel hurt or unloved? Do you try to conform to the person's rules so he or she will accept you?

WRAP-UP *5 minutes*

Questions, comments, prayer.

BELIEVING
THE GOSPEL

BIG IDEA

We have been focusing on the ways we minimize the gospel—the negative. This lesson turns our attention to the positive: what remedies has God given in the gospel to keep us from shrinking the cross and depending on our own effort?

LESSON OVERVIEW

I. BIBLE CONVERSATION	Read and talk about the passage(s) [10 min]
II. ARTICLE	Read *Believing the Gospel* together [10 min]
III. DISCUSSION	Process concepts together [5 min]
IV. EXERCISE	Apply the concepts using a specific exercise [20 min]
V. WRAP-UP	Final thoughts and prayer [5 min]

BIBLE CONVERSATION *10 minutes*

This passage establishes a biblical foundation for the concepts in this lesson. Warning: this is more like an exercise that poses as a discussion. You need to understand the goal if you want to lead the conversation in the right direction, so here is some help. In this text, Peter says we have everything we need for life and godliness (vv. 3–4). Then he proceeds to list a bunch of things we should be doing in light of this reality (vv. 5–8). You are going to stop reading after verse 8 and then ask the group how they are doing according to this list. Most people will express struggle. Then you will ask them why this is such a challenge. They will likely list all kinds of very legitimate reasons and explanations. What they are not likely to identify as the problem is the exact thing Peter does identify in verse 9, namely, that they have drifted away from the gospel. It's a punch line; so don't give it away until you get there! This is one of those things that need to smack us in the face.

INTRO QUESTION   We are going to look at a great passage but before we do, let me ask you a question: when you envision the kind of person you want to be spiritually, what kinds of things do you see? Another way to put it might be the question, in what ways do you want to grow spiritually?

TRANSITION TO PASSAGE   This is a great list. Perhaps we could summarize our desires as "being fruitful and effective in our faith." I use those words because those are the words Peter uses in the passage we are going to read. Peter lays out a set of instructions for the Christian life. It's like a progression of spiritual maturity.

READ   Let's look at it together. It is in 2 Peter 1 (Have someone read 2 Peter 1:3–8 aloud.)

ASK   Peter says in verse 8 that if we do the things mentioned in verses 5–7, we will be fruitful and effective in our faith (which is really what we all want). How do you think you are doing according to this list? If you compared yourself to the qualities listed here, how would you rate your progress?

ASK   Why is it difficult sometimes to grow spiritually? What challenges do you face when it comes to doing the things Peter lists or becoming the person you want to be?

Make a list of the reasons people give.

ASK   I would say many of the same things. These are all real challenges. But Peter identifies something else altogether. Read verse 9. (Have someone read the verse aloud.) According to Peter, what is the real reason we don't grow spiritually?

TRANSITION TO ARTICLE   This goes back to what we talked about in the first lesson—that the gospel is not the entry point but rather the pathway of spiritual life. The article we're about to read is going to explain further how the gospel changes us.

ARTICLE *10 minutes*

Ask your group to turn to the article *Believing the Gospel* in their Participant's Guide and read it aloud together, taking turns at the paragraph breaks.

DISCUSSION *5 minutes*

There isn't really a formal discussion for this article because the concepts are worked out in the exercise. However, it is a good idea to make sure people understand the concepts in the article. You may just ask if anyone has any clarifying questions, or you may ask a few questions to see if people are tracking with the article. Either way, once you feel good about it, get to the exercise. It will take some time.

TRANSITION TO EXERCISE There are some really important concepts in this article that we need to process personally, so I want to take some time to do this exercise. It will help us understand how we can apply the gospel more effectively to our lives.

EXERCISE: Orphans vs. Children
20 minutes

1. Turn to the *Orphans vs. Children* exercise

2. Read aloud the paragraph at the top.

3. Give people a few minutes to complete the chart individually.

4. Sharing (Left Side): I want everyone to share what they recognized about themselves. Starting with the left side, let's go around the room and share our top two or three "orphan" tendencies.

After everyone has shared, pick the three or four most common bullet points for your group. For each one, ask these questions:

`ASK` How does feeling this way affect how you relate to God and others?

`ASK` How does this tendency reveal a fundamental unbelief in the truths of the gospel (specifically, adoption or passive righteousness)?

5. Sharing (Right Side): Now let's go around the room starting with the right side. I'd like each of you to share the two or three ways in which you want to grow in living out of your gospel identity.

After everyone has shared, pick the three or four most common bullet points for your group. For each one, ask these questions:

`ASK` How would this change the way you relate to God and others?

`ASK` How does the gospel (specifically, adoption or passive righteousness) empower you to grow in this way?

WRAP-UP *5 minutes*

Questions, comments, prayer.

LAW & GOSPEL

BIG IDEA

We are still thinking about how the gospel interacts with our lives, but now we are doing it by considering the gospel's relationship to the law. What is the law? Does God expect me to obey it? What is the purpose of the law? How does the law help me to believe the gospel? How does the gospel help me to obey the law? These are the questions before us in this lesson.

LESSON OVERVIEW

I. BIBLE CONVERSATION	Read and talk about the passage(s) [10 min]
II. ARTICLE	Read *The Law and the Gospel* together [10 min]
III. DISCUSSION	Process concepts together [15 min]
IV. EXERCISE	Apply the concepts using a specific exercise [20 min]
V. WRAP-UP	Final thoughts and prayer [5 min]

BIBLE CONVERSATION *10 minutes*

This week's passage (Rom. 10:1–4) speaks of Christ being "the end of the law." The question you want your group to wrestle with is what does this mean? Does it mean God's law doesn't matter anymore? Hint: the answer is no, but if your group heads in that direction in the Bible conversation, you can let it slide because the article will bring the needed correction. The point of this Bible conversation is not to "solve the passage" but simply to get people thinking about the issue. So, if the questions only lead to more questions, that's good! The article will have plenty of answers.

SETUP   We have been talking about the gospel. One major dilemma or challenge in understanding the gospel centers on the role of the law—all the commands and expectations God places upon us. Let's start our conversation by reading and talking about a passage where Paul mentions this issue.

READ   Have someone read Romans 10:1–4 out loud.

ASK   What two types of righteousness seem to be contrasted in this passage?

ASK   What does this passage say about Jesus and his relationship to the law?

TRANSITION TO ARTICLE   This passage says that Christ is "the end of the law." But Jesus also said we're not to dismiss the law (Matt. 5:17–19). Which is it? What are we supposed to do with the law? Hopefully, this article will answer our questions along these lines. Let's read it together and then talk more about this.

ARTICLE *10 minutes*

Ask your group to turn to the article *The Law & The Gospel* in their Participant's Guide and read it aloud together, taking turns at the paragraph breaks.

TRANSITION TO DISCUSSION   We don't usually talk about "the law," at least not like people did in Paul's day. So let's talk about these concepts and see how they relate to our context.

DISCUSSION *15 minutes*

These questions are aimed at helping everyone understand the concepts in the article and connect them to their own beliefs and actions.

ASK   Having read the article, how would you summarize the way the law and the gospel work together?

ASK The author of the article talks about feeling like "you ought to be a better Christian." Where do you feel like you ought to be doing better right now?

ASK How does it feel to live under this sense of "ought" or "should"?

TRANSITION TO EXERCISE The Bible uses the phrase "under the law" to describe the experience of living our spiritual lives on the treadmill of what we "ought" to be or do. Here's the tension: If we try to live by the law, we are not living in light of the gospel. But if we dismiss the law altogether, we don't experience the gospel's power to help us obey the law. This tension affects the way we read the Bible, so I want us to do an exercise to help us keep these things in their proper places as we read the Bible and follow Christ.

EXERCISE: The Gospel Grid & the Law
20 minutes

1. Turn to the *Gospel Grid & the Law* exercise with your group.

2. Read the explanation aloud. (Stop at the Practice section.)

3. Together, work through a few passages from the Practice section using the "gospel grid."

WRAP-UP *5 minutes*

Questions, comments, prayer.

REPENTANCE

BIG IDEA

This lesson deals with repentance. In our culture, this usually sounds like a bad thing—like getting called into the boss's office on Friday afternoon. Far from being bad or unusual, biblical repentance is the norm for gospel-centered living. Becoming more aware of God's holiness and our sinfulness leads us to repent and believe the gospel of Jesus. We are constantly turning from our performing and pretending so that we may live as sons and daughters. Biblical repentance frees us from our own devices and makes a way for the power of the gospel to bear fruit in our lives. But sin taints our repentance and robs us of its fruit. So our aim in this lesson is to (1) expose the ways in which we practice counterfeit repentance and (2) move us toward genuine repentance.

LESSON OVERVIEW

I. BIBLE CONVERSATION	Read and talk about the passage(s) [10 min]
II. ARTICLE	Read *Lifestyle Repentance* together [20 min]
III. DISCUSSION	Process concepts together [15 min]
IV. EXERCISE	Apply the concepts using a specific exercise [20 min]
V. WRAP-UP	Final thoughts and prayer [5 min]

BIBLE CONVERSATION *10 minutes*

This text introduces the topic of repentance and will hopefully provoke some good questions. You do not need to figure everything out about this passage. Just allow it to get the conversation going.

INTRO QUESTION   When the sins of others affect or bother you, what kinds of things do you need to see in them before you feel better about them or forgive them? *(I want them to feel bad about it, apologize, reap the consequences, turn from their sin so they can experience God's grace, etc.)*

TRANSITION   We are usually a mixed bag of desires when it comes to people's sin. Sometimes we really want what is best for them. Sometimes we just want to feel better about ourselves. We're going to read a passage that shows Paul's desire for the Corinthians in this area.

READ   Have someone read 2 Corinthians 7:5–13.

ASK   What did Paul want from the Corinthians?

Godly grief that leads to repentance.

ASK   Why did he want this?

For their good and progress in the faith.

ASK   What was the fruit of repentance in their lives? (vv. 7, 11)

ASK   How did their repentance affect Paul?

He was comforted by God, not merely justified in his rebuke.

ARTICLE 20 minutes

Ask your group to turn to the article *Lifestyle Repentance* in their Participant's Guide and read it aloud together, taking turns at the paragraph breaks.

DISCUSSION 15 minutes

ASK   What stood out most to you in this article?

ASK   How would you explain the difference between true and false repentance in your own words?

ASK   Do you see yourself tending more toward remorse or resolution?

ASK   What do you think are some evidences or marks of true repentance?

TRANSITION TO EXERCISE   For this to really take root in us, we have to talk about how we can practice genuine repentance in our lives. We are going to do an exercise that will help us identify counterfeit repentance and move us toward true repentance.

EXERCISE: Practicing Repentance
20 minutes

This exercise will help your group identify forms of counterfeit repentance and practice genuine repentance—and we mean "practice" in a very literal sense. The group will be processing common responses of false repentance (and the underlying heart sins) in an effort to determine how people can truly repent in specific situations. You are practicing something that needs to be lived out in real life. Because repentance often carries a negative connotation, you will need to remind your group that it is good and normal. This exercise is an expression of a loving community.

---

1. Turn to the *Practicing Repentance* exercise with your group.

2. Read through the instructions given and **work through** the exercise with your group.

WRAP-UP *5 minutes*
Questions, comments, prayer.

HEART IDOLATRY

BIG IDEA

We've said that the Christian walk consists of two repeated steps: repentance and faith. In Lesson Five, we dealt with repentance. Now we turn our attention to the topic of faith. Remember, we grow through believing the gospel. That's the emphasis of this week's discussion and exercise. Easy enough, right? This week's goal is to take "believing the gospel" out of the abstract and make it concrete.

LESSON OVERVIEW

I. BIBLE CONVERSATION	Read and talk about the passage(s) [10 min]
II. ARTICLE	Read *Heart Idolatry* together [10 min]
III. DISCUSSION	Process concepts together [30 min]
IV. WRAP-UP	Final thoughts and prayer [5 min]

BIBLE CONVERSATION *10 minutes*

READ   Have someone read Mark 1:15.

SAY   If Jesus had a bumper sticker (which he would not do!), it would say, "Repent and believe, for the kingdom of heaven is at hand." This was his tagline and the main subject of his teaching.

ASK   What do you think Jesus meant when he said, "Repent and believe?" What was he calling people to?

ASK According to this verse, what exactly are we to believe?

TRANSITION TO ARTICLE The article we're about to read focuses on what it means to believe the gospel and how that produces growth in our lives. Let's read it together.

ARTICLE *10 minutes*

Ask your group to turn to the article *Heart Idolatry* in their Participant's Guide and read it aloud together, taking turns at the paragraph breaks.

TRANSITION TO DISCUSSION Let's talk about the concept of heart idols, and especially *our* heart idols.

DISCUSSION *30 minutes*

ASK First of all, does everyone understand the concept of heart idols?

If anyone answers no, go back and read that section of the article again.

ASK Using the list in the article, which one or two would you say are your biggest heart idols?

Have everyone share.

ASK How does this idol manifest itself in your life? In other words, what surface sins are driven by that idol?

The way to deal with heart idols is to apply the gospel to our specific issues. Let's talk about how we can apply the gospel to our heart idols. *Walk through the following questions with different people in the group, applying the gospel communally to the various heart idols that have been identified.*

ASK How do you see your heart idols failing you?

ASK How does the gospel "deliver" in this area? (How does it actually satisfy your desires or meet your needs more fully than your idols?)

What do you need to receive by faith from the gospel in order to defeat the power of these idols in your life? In other words, what specific biblical truths do you need to "really believe" to combat the idolatries of your heart? Do you find it difficult to believe these truths? Why?

ASK How do your heart idols undermine your ability to love?

ASK How does the gospel free you to love others well?

WRAP-UP *5 minutes*

Questions, comments, prayer.

In your prayer time, focus on "praying the gospel into each other"—that is, praying specifically that the truths of the gospel would defeat the power of the unique idols in each person's life.

MISSION

BIG IDEA

The gospel is simultaneously at work in us and through us. Inwardly, our desires and motives are being changed as we repent and believe the gospel. As we experience Christ's love in this way, we are compelled to engage those around us with the same kind of redemptive love. God's grace brings renewal everywhere, in us and through us.

LESSON OVERVIEW

I. BIBLE CONVERSATION	Read and talk about the passage(s) [10 min]
II. ARTICLE	Read *The Gospel Propels Us Outward* together [10 min]
III. DISCUSSION	Process concepts together [15 min]
IV. EXERCISE	Apply the concepts using a specific exercise [15 min]
V. WRAP-UP	Final thoughts and prayer [5 min]

BIBLE CONVERSATION *10 minutes*

This passage establishes the biblical foundation for this lesson's major concept. The challenge, as it has been all along, is to get past what we believe or agree to "on paper" and see how we fail to live out that belief in real life. You won't get there in a short discussion of these verses but, coupled with the article and exercise, this passage will serve as a good "mirror" by which we can see our actual lives.

READ   Read Galatians 5:13–15 aloud two or three times.

ASK   How is it possible to use our freedom as an opportunity to sin? What are some things that keep us from serving one another as this passage instructs?

TRANSITION TO ARTICLE   What does all this have to do with the gospel or gospel-centered living? Our tendency is to think of transformation as a personal, inward reality. It is that, but it is also an outward, expressed reality. This article will explain that in more depth.

ARTICLE *10 minutes*

Ask your group to turn to the article *The Gospel Propels Us Outward* in their Participant's Guide and read it aloud together, taking turns at the paragraph breaks.

TRANSITION TO DISCUSSION   We are going to be working with this diagram for the next few lessons, so let's spend some time talking about these concepts.

DISCUSSION *15 minutes*

ASK   How many of you feel like the Christian life—especially mission—has become a duty instead of a joyful overflow? What do you think causes that in your life?

ASK   How do you respond when you lack motivation for mission: legalism (obey even though you don't feel like it) or license (don't obey at all)?

TRANSITION TO EXERCISE   Okay, let's see if we can relate this to our actual lives. We are going to look at a series of questions that I want you to answer in the context of your life. Feel free to ask questions of the group if you get stuck. We can help each other work through this if we need to. When we're done, we'll share and process some of our answers together. The most important thing in these exercises is to be honest with yourself. Don't hold back in your answers because you think you might have to read them to everyone. I won't make you read anything you don't want to read, although the more you share, the more you will get out of it.

EXERCISE *15 minutes*

Turn to the exercise *Getting to the Heart of Mission.*

Note: "Mission" is broadly defined here as anything that brings gospel-centered renewal/redemption to people, places, and cultures.

Give people enough time to answer the questions on their own. After people have completed the exercise, use these questions to encourage some sharing:

ASK   How many of your situations involve a co-worker? Neighbor? Family member? Friend? Other?

This will give everyone a chance to share without having to say a whole lot. It will also you give you an idea of how many people were able to identify something.

ASK   Ask for a volunteer (or pick one). Take the person's situation and have the group work through it by applying the gospel to the person's barriers. Ask the group how the gospel addresses the emotional, physical, intellectual, and spiritual barriers to mission in this person's situation?

Repeat with other situations as you have time.

TRANSITION TO WRAP-UP   This has been really good. It helps us to see mission not as an obligation, but as a natural outworking of the gospel. I can address my lack of mission not by addressing mission, but by addressing my unbelief in the gospel. In the next couple of lessons we will apply this concept to conflict and forgiveness.

WRAP-UP *5 minutes*

Questions, comments, prayer.

DON'T FORGET: *I'm going to ask you to complete a short exercise before you come next time. It is listed in Lesson 8, under* Getting to the Heart of Forgiveness.

FORGIVENESS

BIG IDEA

The gospel that works in us always works through us. It shows its power in our relationships and actions. One key way this happens is when we forgive others biblically.

LESSON OVERVIEW

I. BIBLE CONVERSATION	Read and talk about the passage(s) [10 min]
II. ARTICLE	Read *The Gospel Empowers Us to Forgive* together [10 min]
III. EXERCISE	Apply the concepts using a specific exercise [40 min]
IV. WRAP-UP	Final thoughts and prayer [5 min]

BIBLE CONVERSATION *10 minutes*

The point in this passage is pretty straightforward. But, of course, simple does not equal easy.

`SETUP`   The passage we are going to read tonight is pretty straightforward. It's one of Jesus' parables. So as we read, look for the point of the story.

`READ`   Read Matthew 18:21–35 out loud.

`ASK`   Okay, what is the point of the story?

`ASK`   If you had to explain what it means to forgive someone, what would you say?

`TRANSITION TO ARTICLE`   Forgiveness isn't easy. This article will explain the biblical concept of forgiveness, and then we'll get into the homework I gave you last time.

ARTICLE *10 minutes*

Ask your group to turn to the article *The Gospel Empowers us to Forgive* in their Participant's Guide and read it aloud together, taking turns at the paragraph breaks.

`ASK`   Having read that, what seem to be the important aspects of forgiveness?

`TRANSITION TO DISCUSSION`   Okay, let's get to the hard part: how do we do at forgiving others?

EXERCISE *40 minutes*

*You gave **the first half of this exercise**—Getting to the Heart of Forgiveness—to your group last week, and they should have answered the questions on their own.*

`ASK`   What did you guys think of the homework? Was it hard to do, insightful, convicting, etc.? Why?

ASK   Ask someone to share his or her answer to question 2, and then do the same for questions 3–6.

You want people to share some of what they wrote down, but they don't need to share all of their answers, and they definitely don't need to use people's names.

Application Questions

*This is **the second part of the exercise**, which you will do as a group. Taking some of the situations that have been shared, the group will talk about how the gospel can empower us to forgive in those situations. This applies the truths you've been talking about for weeks to this important issue. Here are the questions.*

1. Explain how the gospel can enable you to have compassion and genuine love toward people you need to forgive. (Be specific to your situations.)

2. Describe some of the specific steps of love you will take in these relationships. This is not theory! We are, as a group, helping each other to live out the gospel. We will provide accountability toward that goal.

TRANSITION TO WRAP-UP   This has been really good. It's hard to do this stuff, but this is what "faith working through love" is all about. Let's take some time to pray for one another as we pursue the people we need to love and forgive this week.

WRAP-UP *5 minutes*

Questions, comments, prayer.

CONFLICT

BIG IDEA

Conflict is something we all experience (regularly), but often handle in very fleshly ways. The gospel gives us a pattern and a means to healthy conflict resolution.

LESSON OVERVIEW

I. BIBLE CONVERSATION	Read and talk about the passage(s) [10 min]
II. ARTICLE	Read *The Gospel Helps Us Fight Fairly* together [10 min]
III. DISCUSSION	Process concepts together [10 min]
IV. EXERCISE	Apply the concepts using a specific exercise [30 min]
V. WRAP-UP	Final thoughts and prayer [5 min]

BIBLE CONVERSATION *10 minutes*

`READ`　Read Galatians 2:11–14 aloud.

`ASK`　Why was Peter (Cephas) in the wrong? What was Paul's motive in confronting Peter?

`TRANSITION TO ARTICLE`　This article will take us deeper into how (and how not) to handle conflict in our relationships.

ARTICLE *10 minutes*

Ask your group to turn to the article *The Gospel Helps Us Fight Fairly* in their Participant's Guide and read it aloud together, taking turns at the paragraph breaks.

DISCUSSION *10 minutes*

Okay, let's see where we land on this spectrum.

 ASK Who is an attacker? Who is a withdrawer?

ASK What things on the two lists in the article did you most identify with? (That is, how do you specifically tend to attack or withdraw?)

ASK Why do you think we handle conflict this way?

TRANSITION TO EXERCISE I think this exercise will help us not only discover why we attack or withdraw, but also how to move toward a gospel-centered approach to conflict.

EXERCISE *30 minutes*

Turn to the *Gospel-Centered Conflict Resolution* exercise and read through the chart together with your group.

ASK Ask if there are any questions about the chart. Then give everyone time to complete the questions on their own.

SHARING After people have completed the questions, ask individuals in the group to talk about their responses. As people share about their situations and the ways they have wrongly dealt with them, invite the group to help apply the gospel to those situations. In other words, what will gospel-driven conflict look like in that particular situation, in contrast to attacking or withdrawing?

WRAP-UP *5 minutes*

Questions, comments, prayer.

mission
propelled by good news

At Serge we believe that mission begins through the gospel of Jesus Christ bringing God's grace into the lives of believers. This good news also sustains and empowers us to cross nations and cultures to bring the gospel of grace to those whom God is calling to himself.

As a cross-denominational, reformed, sending agency with more than 200 missionaries and 25 teams in 5 continents, we are always looking for people who are ready to take the next step in sharing Christ, through:

- **Short-term Teams**: One- to two-week trips oriented around serving overseas ministries while equipping the local church for mission

- **Internships:** Eight-week to nine-month opportunities to learn about missions through serving with our overseas ministry teams

- **Apprenticeships:** Intensive 12–24 month training and ministry opportunities for those discerning their call to cross-cultural ministry

- **Career:** One- to five-year appointments designed to nurture you for a lifetime of ministry

---

Serge Grace at the Fray   **Visit us online at: serge.org/mission**

www.newgrowthpress.com

spiritual
renewal
resources for you

Disciples who are motivated and empowered by grace to reach out to a broken world are handmade, not mass-produced. Serge intentionally grows disciples through curriculum, discipleship experiences, and training programs.

Resources for Every Stage of Growth

Serge offers grace-based, gospel-centered studies for every stage of the Christian journey. Every level of our materials focuses on essential aspects of how the Spirit transforms and motivates us through the gospel of Jesus Christ.

- **101**: The Gospel-Centered Series
  Gospel-centered studies on Christian growth, community, work, parenting, and more.
- **201**: The Gospel Transformation Series
  These studies go a step deeper into gospel transformation, involve homework and more in-depth Bible study
- **301**: The Sonship Course and Serge Individual Mentoring

Mentored Sonship

For more than 25 years Serge has been discipling ministry leaders around the world through our Sonship course to help them experience the freedom and joy of having the gospel transform every part of their lives. A personal discipler will help you apply what you are learning to the daily struggles and situations you face, as well as, model what a gospel-centered faith looks and feels like.

Discipler Training Course

Serge's Discipler Training Course helps you gain biblical understanding and practical wisdom you need to disciple others so they experience substantive, lasting growth in their lives. Available for onsite training or via distance learning, our training programs are ideal for ministry leaders, small group leaders or those seeking to grow in their ability to disciple effectively.

𝒮𝑒𝓇𝑔𝑒 Grace at the Fray   **Find more resources at serge.org**

resources and mentoring
for every stage of
growth

Every day around the world, Serge teams help people develop and deepen a living, breathing, growing relationship with Jesus. We help people connect with God in ways that are genuinely grace-motivated and increase desire and ability to reach out to others. No matter where you are along the way, we have a series that is right for you.

101: The *Gospel-Centered* Series

Our *Gospel-Centered* series is simple, deep, and transformative. Each *Gospel-Centered* lesson features an easy-to-read article and provides challenging discussion questions and application questions. Best of all, no outside preparation on the part of the participants is needed! They are perfect for small groups, those who are seeking to develop "gospel DNA" in their organizations and leaders, and contexts where people are still wrestling with what it means to follow Jesus.

201: The *Gospel Transformation* Series

Our *Gospel Transformation* studies take the themes introduced in our 101-level materials and expand and deepen them. Designed for those seeking to grow through directly studying Scripture each *Gospel Transformation* lesson helps participants grow in the way they understand and experience God's grace. Ideal for small groups, individuals who are ready for more, and one-on-one mentoring, *Gospel Identity*, *Gospel Growth*, and *Gospel Love* provide substantive material, in easy-to-use, manageable sized studies.

The *Sonship* Course and Individual Mentoring from Serge

Developed for use with our own missionaries and used for over 25 years with thousands of Christian leaders in every corner of the world, Sonship sets the standard for whole-person, life transformation through the gospel. Designed to be used with a mentor, or in groups ready for a high investment with each other, each lesson focuses on the type of "inductive heart study" that brings about change from the inside out.

Serge Grace at the Fray

Visit us online at serge.org

www.newgrowthpress.com